Series:
ALA Studies in Librarianship
Number 5

Influencing Students toward Media Center Use

AN EXPERIMENTAL INVESTIGATION IN MATHEMATICS

RON BLAZEK
School of Library Science
Florida State University

American Library Association
Chicago 1975

Library of Congress Cataloging in Publication Data

Blazek, Ron.
  Influencing students toward media center use.

  (ALA studies in librarianship; no. 5)
  Includes bibliographical references.
  1. Instructional materials centers.
2. Mathematics—Study and teaching (Secondary). I. Title.
II. Series: American Library Association. ALA Studies
in librarianship; no. 5.
QA11.B617   510'.7'12   75-26769
ISBN 0-8389-0201-4

Printed in the United States of America

Contents

Contents

Contents

viii

Contents

Tables

Figures

Preface

In the school year 1969–1970, in partial fulfillment of the requirements for the Ph.D. in Library Science, the author undertook an experimental study at the University of Illinois Laboratory School, the objective being to measure the amount of teacher influence on student use of the library. In conducting this experiment, which dealt with the use of nonrequired materials in mathematics, the interface between teacher and media specialist was examined and much data was uncovered. This proved to be fruitful in providing a means by which one could interpret professional responsibilities as they relate to the development and maintenance of an effective school media program.

This work grew out of that earlier academic effort having been updated and treated in a broader context. It is intended to aid individuals, school media specialists and teachers alike, determine for themselves the nature of their potential contribution in producing student users of school media centers and libraries. The administrative role is considered also and principals should find it. helpful in determining a proper orientation to the media center in the educational process. Support for the school library media center by higher authority is indispensable to its efficient operation, and this support is forthcoming only in instances where the administrator is an enlightened individual. The final chapter is especially helpful in spelling out in concrete terms what each individual can do to stimulate media center use.

It is the author's feeling that the most important feature in a steadily improving educational program is its own dynamism as opposed to the inertia of the traditionalist operation. The latter seems hell-bent on preserving that which was and assumes a defensive posture protective of the customary mediocrity often found in schools. The former, on the other hand, seeks answers to questions and solutions to problems which have been identified in a systematic manner. The reliance in this work is on a scientific approach rather than upon exhortation to point the way toward greater use of the media center. This book is designed to help teachers, media specialists and principals alike to integrate media center resources into the curriculum.

In so doing, this work may serve as a manual for experimentation at the school level. By providing a casebook of the problem (neglect of mathematics materials by student users of the school media center) and detailing the manner by which this problem was attacked and overcome, we hope to provide the insight needed by members of the school staff in order to conduct their own investigations. These individuals assuredly have identified troubling circumstances in the past and more than likely have conjectured upon their causes. What they may need is a good starting point, along with a strong dose of encouragement for any studies they may choose to undertake.

This, of course, makes this work equally valuable to doctoral students interested in using the school for field study. Although the language and style of presentation have been reworked to make it serve the needs of a larger reading audience, and many of the statistical applications and tables have been deleted, the "research tone" is unmistakably present. Prospective investigators seeking to conceptualize a suitable framework for attacking their problems should benefit considerably and will be especially interested in chapters 1, 3, and 4, while media specialists, teachers, and principals will find chapters 1 and 5 to be most useful to their practice.

The Media Specialist–Teacher Partnership: Study and Speculation

> Every good librarian knows that if a teacher aids in the choice of
> books, offers suggestions for use, and is notified when the books
> are ready for use, those books will circulate. Student use of a
> school library is very often motivated by an enthusiastic library-
> minded teacher.[1]

Those who work in the field of education are well acquainted with the
type of journal article from which the above words are quoted. Such
writings promulgate basic assumptions of the teacher's role in the educational process, are numerous, and usually reflect the author's opinion which
has been formed through classroom experience, through education courses,
or, cyclically, through perusal of similar contemporary journal articles.

The quest for truth, however, is not best served through uncontrolled or
undirected observations or adherence to a belief which may not emanate
from supportable theory. Too frequently, such writings tend to overlook
many variables or to consider them in an inadequate manner. To be sure,
the assumptions generally are logical and in many cases employ a keen
sense of deduction. What is needed to give substance to their allegations is
research properly designed to provide a real comprehension of the situation.

Although the effects of the teacher's interactions with the media center
have been studied in the past in several ways and with varying degrees of
sophistication, it is clear that much more work is needed to shed light on
this complex phenomenon. The value of this undertaking is pointed out by
Jean Lowrie[2] in a comprehensive review of research in school librarianship
which she prepared as a paper for the research conference held at the
University of Illinois in 1967. One of the topics which she identified as
needing further research was the role of the teacher and the utilization of
library services and materials.

This is still true today, some eight years later, and we see a strong plea for cooperation between teacher and media specialist in the newly published AASL-AECT standards, *Media Programs: District and School*. What this present work seeks to show is tangible results of such cooperative endeavors in terms of their ultimate success: motivating and creating student users of the school library media center. In our concern with the teacher, the media specialist, and the student, we ascribe to each one a degree of influence affecting the other two in some measurable way. That this influence can and should be measured with some degree of precision is the element which distinguishes research from speculative, opinionated commentary.

The Opinions

Of course, it is important to know what the practitioners in a field feel their role to be to understand the reasoning employed in reaching decisions and formulating policy. To gain a thorough familiarity with the opinions of both teachers and media specialists regarding their proper roles, the author carefully examined numerous publications on the topic representative of the literature of both education and librarianship.

Rossoff, in his work on the high school library, "recognizes the subject teacher as the prime mover in any educational undertaking, but particularly so in the case of the school library."[3] He refers to the understanding and support of the classroom teacher as the first of three components essential to the success of the library program, since it is the teacher who most strongly determines the quality and extent of library use by pupils. The second essential is the administrator, and third is the cooperating librarian.[4]

A report on the use of a multimedia center in a Kansas elementary school contains this comment from a teacher, "We create a desire to solve a problem, which opens up many questions. Thus we find that learning takes place as naturally as eating follows hunger."[5] Grazier, in writing for the benefit of school principals, goes so far as to state that "any curricular innovation which requires learning beyond the confines of a single textbook affects the library and the librarian."[6]

Cole concludes his description of library enrichment of the curriculum by saying that "in the final analysis, it is the classroom teacher who actually sees that library resources are used extensively, if they are."[7] He follows this statement with a plea for cooperation between teachers and librarians in order to benefit the child's learning situation.

The element of cooperation is the point upon which role interpreters generally agree. Indeed, there is very little disagreement among observers with regard to any aspect, but none is mentioned with such consistency and emphasis as is cooperation. Most of these writings then take a pragmatic turn and suggest ways in which the teacher may improve his library effectiveness; they almost become manuals for achieving a proper role with respect to the utilization of the media center.

Klohn states that "what use high school teachers make of the library depends upon their understanding of the curricular needs of their students and upon their methods of instruction." She then offers six suggestions for effective use: using librarian-made bibliographies, requesting that materials in short supply be placed on reserve, using student permits to the library when a visit is needed, using specific references in the case of average students, requesting that the librarian locate materials and set them aside for class visits, and having materials sent to the classroom for projects of longer duration.[8]

Beachner suggests five new roles for the teacher all of which involve collaboration with the librarian and use of the library: environmental designer, guide and consultant, team teacher, innovator in evaluation, and expert in children's materials.[9]

Taylor states that "the subject teacher who not only recommends background library books for his lesson but also brings them into the classroom with him and signs them out on the spot is teaching more than his subject."[10] He then discusses six types of library use by the teacher: research approach, background reinforcement, topical lecturette, unit procedure, problem method of learning, and supervised study.[11]

An unsigned article appearing in the *Instructor* over a decade ago suggested that teachers converse with the librarian both informally and through committees to inform her of classroom activities.[12] Holmes agrees and restates the case for careful cooperative planning, maintaining that teachers should keep librarians informed "concerning the levels of readiness for independent learning."[13]

McJenkin feels that the "program of service is becoming a joint responsibility of its users,"[14] and then goes on to describe certain basic areas of librarian-teacher cooperation: selection of library materials, promotion and planning for their effective use, provision of meaningful instruction in the use of the library, and stimulation of pupil learning experiences.[15] She explains that the "vitality of any library program will be intensified when teachers become personally involved in using and improving the library, when they conscientiously motivate their students to use its facilities, and when they stress the importance of and a respect for its services."[16]

It is readily seen that opinion-type commentary regarding roles does not differ markedly from one article to another. Most authors promulgate ideas acceptable at the time, whether or not they have a solid basis. They generally structure their responses on the basis of visceral reactions to the situation as it has affected them personally. Klohn and Taylor are both school media specialists who represent the practical but rather limited view, giving their impressions of successful experiences in their own media centers. McJenkin, as a supervisor of school libraries, represents more breadth but still embraces her categories of teacher-media specialist interaction through isolated examples drawn from the experiences of her past associations. Holmes, a university professor, discusses the challenges ahead in general terms, urging the librarian to involve himself and to keep abreast of latest developments. Teachers and media people alike identify the need for cooperation and cite considerations which are similar in nature.

Additional observations usually emanate from the personal experiences of the writers. James reiterates several of the points and adds that the teacher can be assigned to the library to assist and supervise.[17] Swanson feels that teachers should schedule longer time blocks for library work under a system of flexible scheduling,[18] while Mount refers to the need for conferences between individual faculty members and the librarian.[19]

Obviously, the body of literature has been ample in the past and just as obvious is its distinctive shortcoming. Notably lacking in this speculative commentary is a consideration in quantifiable terms of the degree of influence wielded by either the teacher or the media specialist in producing student library users. The question as to how much one could reasonably expect to accomplish working with students in either capacity is enshrouded in vague and often insignificant pleas for further efforts, encapsulated by the call for lubrication of the cooperative machinery. The very difficult task of conducting a penetrating analysis of variables is generally left undone.

The Teacher and the Media Center—A Simplified Model

To better understand the relationships involved in the process of interaction, it is necessary to examine the conceptual framework as it appears to exist. Drawing upon his experience as both a teacher and school media specialist as well as his careful examination of the literature of the field, the author sees the pattern of library involvement by the teacher as being represented adequately by a six-step model. Although somewhat oversimplified (the entire context of the problem being presented in only six categorical heads), one cannot help but feel that if this model is properly understood, the phenomenon can be studied in an effective manner. The six steps are identified as:

1. Teacher's background and experience with the media center
2. Teacher's attitude toward the media center
3. Teacher's participation in media center activities

4

4. Teacher's utilization of the center's resources
5. Teacher's influence on students as measured by student use
6. Student benefits derived from use of the media center.

TEACHER'S BACKGROUND AND EXPERIENCE WITH THE MEDIA CENTER

As the first component in the pattern of teacher involvement, the vital nature of this element is obvious. In utilizing library resources as first a student, then an instructor, familiarity is established with the media center as an educational enterprise either worthy or unworthy of support. Thus the potential for full utilization of resources in the future is determined. Of course, it is true that a teacher with a somewhat deprived background or unfortunate past experiences can rise above such adversity in his subsequent recognition of the value of the center for his students. In this case, the challenge obviously resides in the determination of the desirable experiences leading to favorable attitudes.

TEACHER'S ATTITUDE TOWARD THE MEDIA CENTER

A healthy attitude toward the media center in the school is usually held by the teacher who by previous experience has come to realize its potential. Such desirable attitudes may have been inculcated at any stage in the development of the individual professional character or may have had their inception in childhood. Involvement with it as a teacher, therefore, is a natural activity. Similarly, negative attitudes emanate from unpleasant or unprofitable experiences, either with individual librarians or inadequate collections. Neutral feelings usually generate from a dearth of experience. Past research has shown that teachers' attitudes are associated to a certain degree with subject specialization, but there is no definitive examination of this relationship.

TEACHER'S PARTICIPATION IN MEDIA CENTER ACTIVITIES

In addition to active engagement in materials selection and collection building, certain teachers strive to cooperate in promotional programs such as book fairs, teas, exhibits and displays. The extent to which a teacher is willing to participate in such activities or special programs is conditioned by the attitudes he holds concerning the value and purpose of the center. This involvement reflects a situation in which the school media center is regarded as an important asset to the instructional program. On the other hand, teachers, like anyone else, do not wish to waste their valuable time in meaningless expenditures of energy. Thus if there is little appreciation

5

for the media center's role in curriculum implementation, then there will be little support for its programs.

Teacher's Utilization of the Center's Resources

If we concede the importance of the three elements, background and experience, favorable attitudes, and active participation in center activities, we are able to comprehend their relationship to the teacher's use of the center's materials in the realization of his instructional objectives. The value of the center is understood and its potential is being exploited in the case of the teacher who makes frequent use of its resources. Evidence shows that teachers in certain subject areas are more likely to fall into this category than are teachers in other subject fields.

Teacher's Influence on Students as Measured by Student Use

Here, the question is posed as to what effect a teacher may have on his students. Obviously, some teachers have very little influence while others are highly stimulating. To measure a teacher's influence necessitates an identification of those qualities or characteristics which can be considered as predictors of effectiveness. Given a teacher who is imbued with the library spirit and who possesses the necessary characteristics of effectiveness, can we expect the influence to extend beyond the classroom into the center? We believe the answer is yes and predicate this study on that basis. In short, an effective teacher who believes in the value of materials and promotes their use *will be able to make media center users of his students.*

Student Benefits Derived from Media Center Use

The final component in the spectrum of teacher-media center interaction is the assessment of the value to the student. Will his grades improve once he becomes a user? Will he be more perceptive or knowledgeable in the subject? In what other ways has the experience been of benefit? These are some of the questions which could be asked if we are not simply to make the assumption that all curriculum-related reading, viewing, and listening activities are good and of benefit to the pupil.

The Present Study

As stated in the preface, the author conducted his study at the University of Illinois Laboratory High School in the year 1969–70, the objective being to examine the educational process. The study thus represents an

6

effort to tie together steps 4 and 5 of the model by providing support for its validity. In effect, the basic assumption for many studies of the past— that the contribution of the school library or media center is conditioned by the use made of its materials by teachers—serves as the premise. Teacher's utilization (step 4) and the resulting influence on students' use (step 5) are therefore explored in depth. To identify the effective teacher and then proceed with a properly controlled investigation of that teacher's influence on student media center behavior was the major task. The result was envisioned as a better understanding of the roles and responsibilities of teachers and school media specialists.

Although data regarding student grades have been collected and are presented, little attempt is made to assess the advantages accruing to students in this regard since the amount of information is limited (step 6 being outside the focus of this effort). Nor will the teacher's library background (step 1), past attitudes (step 2), or past participation in activities (step 3) be evaluated. Rather, this study is a simple representation of the here and now—an effective teacher presently encouraging the use of media center resources in his teaching routine and an analysis of his influence on student use of those materials.

TEACHER EFFECTIVENESS—HYPOTHESIS AND LOGICAL CONSEQUENCES

The major task in constructing a hypothesis for the study was to identify those characteristics which are indicative of teacher effectiveness. From our description of teacher effectiveness in chapter 3, we find that the two traits of a teacher which appear to be of most consequence to students are desirable personality and subject matter expertise. A teacher possessing either or both of these qualities is most likely to be influential, and thereby cause changes in the students' behavioral patterns. This was a logical statement which drew support from the author's previous experience in schools and led to the following hypothesis: *The greater the teacher utilization of media center resources in his teaching, the greater the use of the center by pupils because in their recognition of the teacher as a subject matter authority they will emulate his manner of acquiring knowledge and/or in their regard for him as a desirable personality will seek to please him.*

Several logical consequences are seen to arise from the stated hypothesis. They are:

1. The number of books mentioned or suggested by the teacher in the performance of his teaching function is directly proportional to the amount of pupil circulation of library media.

7

2. Of two teachers alike in every way save for the utilization of library media, the teacher who rates higher in this respect will have pupils to whom greater numbers of materials have circulated.
3. Of two media centers alike in every way save for the extent of teacher utilization of resources, the media center which rates higher in this respect will circulate the greater number of materials to pupils.
4. The heaviest circulation of materials is to pupils enrolled in courses taught by teachers who most often utilize such resources in their teaching.

Each of these logical consequences could be tested for veracity, having been created within the framework of the general hypothesis. They by no means exhaust the number of research possibilities here but serve simply to indicate the potential. For our study, we have chosen logical consequence four, and therefore, it serves as the basis for the design.

LIMITATIONS OF THE STUDY

All research efforts possess certain limitations which should be recognized. Of the several which exist here, the first concerns the sample. Seventeen students of subfreshman (junior high school) level in each of two mathematics classes at the University of Illinois Laboratory High School served as subjects for the study. In addition to being of small size, the sample is admittedly a biased one, representative of neither the entire population of junior high school students nor, necessarily, the population of laboratory school students. At best it may be representative of subfreshman classes at this particular school. The difficulty is similar to that which many other researchers have faced, the fact that the study deals with only one case (school-teacher-subject area) at one given period of time. It is recognized that breadth must be sacrificed for depth, and generalization therefore will not be an easy task. This of course will not be a problem for school staff researchers who are primarily interested in finding answers to problems in their own educational units.

On the plus side, however, there are advantages in the selection of this sample. The fact that the experiment is being conducted on youngsters of above average intelligence and ability helps to isolate a type or category of pupil upon whom the results of teacher utilization can be measured. If the results are positive, then the study may be replicated with pupils of normal ability in the public schools to determine if any differences exist. If, however, results are negative with this group, the chance for positive results with public school youngsters would be lessened considerably. The selection of the sample is covered in greater detail in chapter 3.

A second limitation concerns the search for causes or reasons. The situation involving student acceptance of teacher suggestions is a complex one and differs in various ways with different sets of individuals. Research in these areas has often been vague and inconsistent. The use of two factors, subject matter expertise and desirable personality as components of or prerequisites for teacher influence, comes as a result of a familiarity with past research.

Even so, teacher influence is recognized as only one of several possible causes. Other important considerations are the guidance aspect (giving students bibliographies which are well designed, informative, economical of students' time, and pertinent), pupils' satisfaction with materials, and, finally, the pupils' subject interest. Although it was possible for us to provide a measurement of subject interest and satisfaction, we were unable to remove the factor of guidance from that of teacher influence. Instead, the utilization of the teacher-made bibliographies by pupils is treated as a function of teachers' influence in general. This is explained more fully in chapter 4.

There are at least three additional limitations which we might identify. The objective of the study itself is a limitation in that only the phenomenon of teacher utilization-student use is analyzed, without regard to any ultimate benefits derived from such contact. Also, there may very well be certain long-term effects which are capable of being determined only beyond the arbitrary time designations dictated as the period of involvement.

Still another, perhaps minor, limitation concerns the scope of the data and reflects the possibility that there may have been overlooked some important factors in the characteristics of the teacher or of the students. Two characteristics of the teacher are seen as most important in assessing his or her influence, viz., personality and subject-matter expertise. Similarly, the student is judged on several characteristics deemed pertinent to his or her potential use of media center resources in mathematics: IQ, mathematics achievement score, mathematics grade, interest in mathematics, reading achievement score, father's education, and number of free periods. Other variables, although not considered, may be of importance.

Finally, the limitations of the instruments must be acknowledged. Although the interview schedules and rating scales are carefully structured and a check instituted in the former regarding the accuracy of responses, there are the usual assumptions to be made with respect to the honesty and capacity to recall on the part of the respondents. This receives more detailed treatment in chapter 3.

VALUE OF THE MEDIA CENTER—FOUR VITAL QUESTIONS

Clearly, we have set for ourselves a worthy goal. To understand the potential value of the media center in the educational program as well as the interface between teachers and media specialists is a giant step forward in the development of optimum learning experiences. In so doing we confront directly four questions posed by Knapp[20] which remain unexplained with any degree of finality:

1. What is the extent of the contribution to course work?
2. What is the nature of the contribution to the instructional program?
3. What factors limit the contribution to the instructional program?
4. What should be the contribution to the instructional program?

These we must attempt to answer, since within their framework is found the essence of the school media center. Of course, for our study purposes we were concentrating on the mathematics program as our primary concern, although general principles which relate to all academic subjects surely do follow.

Definition of Terms

Teacher utilization of center resources. Throughout this book the references to teacher utilization shall be interpreted as meaning the extent to which a teacher imparts bibliographic awareness of relevant school media center resources and encourages their use as part of his teaching routine. The author considers a high degree of teacher utilization to be the condition which exists when a teacher employs such methods on a regular basis over a period of time. The term "media center" is the latest descriptor associated with what in the past has been called the library or materials center. We consider such terms to be interchangeable, regarding each one as a proper indication of the school's communication agency and its inherent responsibility to provide materials of various forms and types.

Use of the media center. Pupils' use shall be interpreted as the number of loans ascertained by examination of circulation records. Two categories of pupil use are identified and examined: all media including mathematics and mathematics media only.

User of the media center. A user shall be interpreted as being any pupil in our study who has charged at least one item from the center. Two categories of users are compared: users of any media including mathematics and users of mathematics media.

Purpose of the Book

Characteristic of the most recent and progressive thinking in educational psychology is the concern for the application of scientific principles to the study of human behavior. The educational process is now being analyzed in terms of anticipated outcomes or student behaviors resulting from the techniques employed by the architects of the learning structure. When stated clearly prior to the introduction of a learning activity, these behavioral objectives become powerful tools for evaluation of the success of that activity. In effect, they become powerful tools for the control of human behavior.

This manipulation of behavior, or contingency management, employs reinforcement theory in which one seeks to understand the relationship between the resultant behavior and the environmental events which influenced it. One of the major figures in this area is B. F. Skinner who in 1968 described teaching as the arrangement of contingencies or reinforcements under which students learn.[21] The teacher, therefore, is an important controlling force, one who can shape the behavior of his charges.

The major purpose of the author in writing this book is to shed light on the complex phenomenon of teacher influence and to analyze its potential in developing student users of the school media center. In concentrating on the teacher's library role as part of an earlier academic effort, the natural concomitant proved to be a similar understanding of the educational role of the media specialist. Thus we were able to comprehend the curricular activity of teacher and media specialist and the relationship they have to each other. Our interest, then, is in what influences students to use the media center and in the kind of instruction that can foster such use.

The emphasis on the cause-effect relationship in this study reflects the author's belief in the validity of recent educational theory. It mirrors a profound respect for the teacher as the single most important figure in both establishing new student behavioral patterns and restructuring existing ones. With respect to the interface of the media center and curriculum implementation, the teacher is joined by a powerful ally in the person of the school media specialist. Together they can make a unique contribution to the academic development of the student.

The confusion that exists is exemplified by the following passage by Hartz who laments the fact that results of his survey showed that only 12 percent of 461 high school teachers queried found legitimate academic reasons for using the media center:

> It is tragic, because the teachers should be the ones responsible for encouraging student library use. The subject teacher has a better opportunity to know the interests of her students than does the librarian. Also instruction is better provided by subject teachers in courses when it is needed and when it relates directly to the topics under discussion. If the teacher does not use the library, and know that resources are available there for his students, it is highly unlikely that the students, without teacher stimulation, will use the library.[22]

11

In his keen disappointment, Hartz has presented a very forceful expression of what he feels the teacher's role to be. To gain a better understanding of the school media specialist's responsibility within the educational framework is absolutely necessary to both parties in the future implementation of programs designed to produce students who utilize more fully the center's resources. From the standpoint of efficiency, it is imperative that whatever cooperation is needed between them be undertaken with a fairly precise idea of the type of contribution each is expected to make and the nature of that contribution within the total picture.

School administrators, likewise, need such information. Successful completion of their duties in terms of evaluating the professionals under their charge dictates that they comprehend the professional responsibility of every participant in the learning process. More often than not, this does not hold true in the case of the media center. There appears to be a vague realization that students should be "taught" to use the center, but very little real understanding of how well teachers and media people are performing in this capacity. This is not surprising when one considers the nebulous approach to the problem representative of the professional literature. Indeed, there is very little "to put a handle on." What is needed here is a real awareness in order to establish policy and implement techniques.

Also there are implications for both teacher education and education for school librarianship. Of what importance is subject bibliography in the preparation of those who have chosen to work with youngsters and to what extent should school media specialists be knowledgeable about the curriculum? Possibly much more should be done in the development of interpersonal relations since professional cooperation appears to be such an urgent factor. Of importance to educationists especially, is the amount of influence which is wielded by the teacher in the performance of his daily routines. If it is true that good habits and a proper approach to the learning situation are by-products received by students of the successful teacher, some idea of the nature of the phenomenon should exist. To determine what it is that makes some teachers more influential than others in shaping the opinions and behaviors of their students is an important realization.

Another consideration is the nature of the materials employed. This study deals exclusively with what appears to be an area relatively overlooked in serious research efforts but mentioned frequently in estimating the library role—that of nonrequired materials. Past studies employ required materials and assignments, but very little has been done to interpret the position of supplementary materials in the composition of the media center and even less on the teacher's effective utilization of them. A question may also be asked regarding the form of the materials. If students are more inclined to view a filmstrip than read a book as an optional activity, the nature of that preference should be explored.

A final consideration lies in the choice of mathematics as the subject for investigation. It is felt that the importance of the study would be manifest if the findings can be shown to apply in certain skill areas categorized as minor users of library service by the National Education Association study in 1958.[23] Mathematics is a logical choice. If this study were attempted with a major user such as English, the fact that there is a greater propensity to utilize library resources may work against the investigation in achieving a clear-cut pathway to measurable teacher effects.

Notes

1. Sister Mary Arthur, "The Librarian and the Teacher," *Catholic Library World* 36:89 (Oct. 1964).

2. Jean Lowrie, "A Review of Research in School Librarianship," in Herbert Goldhor, ed., *Research Methods in Librarianship: Measurement and Evaluation* (Monograph no. 8; Champaign, Ill.: Univ. of Illinois Graduate School of Library Science, 1968), p. 63.

3. Martin Rossoff, *The Library in High School Teaching* (2d ed.; New York: Wilson, 1961), p. 7.

4. Ibid., pp. 19–20.

5. M. T. Ward, "Teachers Are Using Multimedia Centers," *Instructor* 77:120 (June–July 1968).

6. Margaret H. Grazier, "The Library and New Programs," *Bulletin of the National Association of Secondary School Principals* 50:23 (Jan. 1966).

7. Tom J. Cole, "Curriculum Enrichment Via the Library," *Peabody Journal of Education* 41:12 (July 1963).

8. Louise L. Klohn, "Six Pointers for Teachers," *Junior Libraries* 5:9–10 (Sept. 1958).

9. Anna B. Beachner, "The Teacher's Role," *Theory Into Practice* 6:37–38 (Feb. 1967).

10. J. E. Taylor, "Library Methods in Subject Teaching," *School Librarian* 10:123–26 (July 1960).

11. Ibid.

12. "The Teacher and the Librarian," *Instructor* 70:83 (Nov. 1960).

13. Doris F. Holmes, "Teachers and Librarians Work Together to Enrich the Curriculum," *School Libraries* 11:14 (Jan. 1962).

14. Virginia McJenkin, "Teacher-Pupil Practices Which Tend to Improve Library Use," *Southeastern Librarian* 14:24 (Spring 1964).

15. Ibid., pp. 24–26.

16. Ibid., p. 27.

17. Donald W. James, "The Teacher and the Library," *Education* 86:547–49 (May 1966).

18. Viola Swanson, "Librarian-Teacher Rapport," *Illinois Education* 53:339 (Apr. 1965).

19. Mary Mount, "The Librarian and Teacher as a Team," *Instructor* 75:88 (Nov. 1965).

20. Patricia B. Knapp, *College Teaching and the College Library* (ACRL Monographs, no. 23; Chicago: American Library Assn., 1959), pp. 3–4.

21. B. F. Skinner, *The Technology of Teaching* (New York: Appleton, 1968).

22. Frederic R. Hartz, "High School Library: A Study in Use, Misuse, and Non-Use," *Clearing House* 38:426 (Mar. 1964).

23. National Education Assn., Research Div. *The Secondary-School Teacher and Library Services* (Research monograph 1958—M1; Washington, DC: The Association, 1958). 37 p.

Research into
Media Center Use

In the past, library research has been conducted in the direction of breaking down the myths associated with the overpowering or disproportionate influence of the library on the life-style of its user. An inquiry of this type was completed by Knapp in 1957.[1] In this carefully constructed and convincing doctoral dissertation, the author shatters the concept of the college library as the "heart of the college," "core of the curriculum," or any other lofty but exaggerated cliche illustrating its position. Her effort was well received by the profession and appeared in brief form two years later as Monograph 23 under the auspices of the Association of College and Research Libraries with the title, *College Teaching and the College Library.*[2]

What Stimulates Student Use?

Knapp assessed the contribution of the Knox College Library to the educational program as manifested in student borrowing and found that influence to be nonexistent. The library was a major consideration in the college experience of only a selected minority of the students. Furthermore, there was evidence to suggest that most college students fail to use their libraries for any purpose, and those who do are not users by their own volition. She succeeded in making a strong case for the need for further research into student motivation.

Another myth breaker was Sister Mary Peter Claver in her 1960 doctoral dissertation entitled "Student and Faculty Use of the Library in Three Secondary Schools."[3] She set out to determine the nature and extent of library use in three Catholic schools, to describe the characteristics of users and nonusers (identifying the factors of sex, grade, IQ, academic rank in class, and reading level), and to indicate certain patterns of library use among teachers and students.

Data were obtained through questionnaire responses of some 2,200 students and 100 teachers concerning their use of the library and their attitudes toward it. Circulation records for a typical library week were examined and supplementary student data were acquired from the schools' records for a study of reader characteristics.

Briefly stated, her findings were that a wide variation exists between teachers of the same subject in their estimation of the importance of library materials, a small percentage of the student body makes regular and frequent library visits, a greater proportion of the better students make use of the school library, and most students use the public library as a complement to the school library or media center. Again, there is little evidence here of the vital role of the school media center in the total program.

It requires no effort on the part of the reader to appreciate the similarity of the positions of the two investigators. Both Knapp and Sister Peter Claver approached the problem in terms of the library's role and both found that role to be greatly exaggerated in importance. The conclusions in both cases were reached as a result of the examination of student circulation records indicating that the library influence is, indeed, a limited one. In fact, Knapp found the effects of library-promoted use to be almost negligible. To overstate the case for the school library was not uncommon (nor undesirable) at the time of its institutional fight for survival, but at present a more accurate assessment of the value of school or college media centers is necessary to deal effectively with perceived shortcomings and thereby facilitate progressive development.

In 1965, Mehit[4] sought to determine whether a real difference existed in the utilization of school library materials and outside reading sources by sixth grade youngsters in 18 selected Ohio schools when compared by physical quarters of the library. Types of libraries were categorized as classroom library, central library, or combination of the two, and for 20 days readings by the pupils were tabulated. He found no significant differences between groups and concluded that mere physical structure is not enough to promote utilization of resources. As did Knapp before him, Mehit recognized the importance of further research into student motivation by urging the formulation of measures to determine successful motivating methods for elementary school library book utilization.

In a later study, Graham[5] attempted to determine the extent to which the instructional materials center was used in 19 Michigan high schools into which had been channeled large federal subsidies from Title II of the Elementary and Secondary Education Act. He hypothesized that after such funding teacher use would have increased, teaching methods would have changed to employ the increased technology, student use would have increased, and students' methods of study would have been altered to incorporate more material as a result of teachers' changed assignments. Although there were some changes in all respects, not one result was statis-

16

tically significant. That is to say the relationship between funding and use of materials was not very great.

Another study focused on socioeconomic characteristics in an attempt to shed light on the inclination of students to use the center. In using such factors as parents' occupation, parents' educational level, and parents' income, Clayton[6] found only slight and insignificant differences between groups. There does, however, tend to be a greater use of reserve books among the students from less affluent backgrounds.

Although Clayton dealt with college students, the implication is clear for any center connected with an educational institution. Students' economic background in itself is no indicator of their disposition to use the materials. Another effort relating primarily to college level students goes even further in its assessment of the inability to predict utilization from student traits. Woods, in his analysis of 25 studies of library use,[7] reported that student characteristics tend not to be important since intelligence is not closely related to library use, and although good students usually borrow more library materials, there were numerous exceptions.

This brings the reader back to the question posited at the beginning of the chapter and which has served as the basic framework for this book. If neither student characteristics nor such elements as physical quarters, ample funding, and increased resources are in any way indicative of the center's use, what factors then are important? Indeed, is there any predictor with a potential for a relatively high degree of scientific accuracy?

As has already been indicated in chapter 1, there is a marked frequency of armchair opinion and speculation in the literature of librarianship and of education with respect to the roles of the teacher and the librarian or media specialist in the utilization of the school media center by students. This is understandable due to the fundamental nature and basic importance of the issue. Moreover, the problem has probably caused more than just a fleeting moment of concern to conscientious school media specialists, anxious to do what needs to be done, but unsure of where or how to start. Many teachers, although they have empathy for their students and are imbued with the spirit of the crusade for quality education, are similarly troubled because they lack library know-how yet are vaguely aware of its potential. If the speculative journal literature has not provided real comprehension of the situation and enlightenment for future active involvement, it has certainly succeeded in keeping us in a state of discomfort due to our awareness of the problem.

More valuable than speculative interpretation in the often frustrating task of becoming a good librarian or teacher is the research. It is clear to the troubled ones, teachers and media specialists alike, that it is necessary to determine the untapped potential of any teaching aid (in this case the media center), and, having accomplished this, to develop a program for its full implementation in the achievement of instructional objectives. Technology, money, physical quarters, and even students' readiness is not enough. To focus on the roles of the two individuals most closely involved with the student's library experience is to recognize the overwhelming importance of the human element in an extremely human situation. For this reason, we feel that the key to student use of the media center lies in the understanding and appreciation by both teacher and media specialist of their professional responsibilities.

Importance of Teacher and Subject

Both Knapp and Sister Peter Claver recognized the value of the teacher in helping students to realize the advantages to be gained by using library resources. Both examined certain characteristics associated with the teacher and attempted to establish relationships to student use. Knapp examined teaching routines in the sense that she recognized a category of library-dependent courses which produced the highest incidence of student borrowing. It was clear that students enrolled in certain courses would tend to use library resources in a disproportionate manner. Sister Peter Claver assessed the attitudes of teachers toward the library, and compared this with their students' use of resources. As is so often the case, she found that teachers do not always practice what they preach, since many indicated that the library was important but apparently did nothing to promote its use.

In 1966, Hostrop conducted a study of academic success and other student characteristics possibly associated with the use of one college library. His results were similar to those of Clayton. Although some of the characteristics are statistically significant, they play only a minor role in quantitative use. Hostrop found instructors to be the chief impellers and the assignment of term papers the primary motivating factor for library use.[8] This is in agreement with the findings of Woods who concluded that the elements upon which there seems to be a general consensus is that the nature of the course and the methods of teaching are major factors in determining use of the center.[9]

A study which figures prominently in the identification of the teacher's role is a research project completed by the National Education Association in 1958.[10] It was in examining this effort, which still remains the most comprehensive survey of secondary school libraries, that the author first felt the need on the part of the profession to gain a greater understanding of the implications of the data.

Five thousand questionnaires were sent to a nationwide sample of teachers, and although the return was relatively small, important correlations were found to exist in several areas affecting the center. Teachers of English, social studies, and science were categorized as major users, while teachers of business education, mathematics, and industrial arts were designated as minor users. It was reported that members of the former group feel the library to be important for teaching effectiveness, make frequent assignments from library materials, and give high ratings to the quality of library materials. The minor users as a group hold contrary views, although individuals within the two groups differ.

Donnelly, in his 1965 dissertation,[11] among other things considered the utilization of materials in eight selected senior high schools and reached the same conclusion regarding subject areas. Teachers of social studies, science, and English were the most frequent users of the instructional materials centers.

At this point it is tempting to state flatly that we can safely identify library-dependent areas in which teachers are moved to become more actively engaged in the media center process. The fact that individuals hold opinions which differ substantially from their colleagues in similar teaching areas (according to the NEA study), however, forces one to resist this natural tendency toward oversimplification, and to a consideration of underlying factors as being pertinent. Therefore, we must examine the teacher more carefully as an individual; and the need for a closer, more structured investigation is apparent.

TEACHER COMMITMENT—THE CHIEF INGREDIENT

The question to be answered, then, is what is present in the composition of media center-oriented teachers and absent in those who make little use of media center resources? At the risk of being simplistic, the critical element appears to be a commitment to the center as an educational aid. A valuable study is a 1961 doctoral dissertation by Saad Mohammed el-Hagrasy[12] in which he investigated teacher characteristics as a predictor for pupils' library use. In this instance, the library background and reading habits of several teachers were compared with the degree of mastery of library skills and with the amount and kind of reading on the part of their pupils. Using two elementary schools each containing four sixth-grade classes, el-Hagrasy investigated these variables, and found a correlation to exist between them. Although his purpose was not to explore causality but rather to devise certain measures of the teacher's role, he showed that pupils tend to emulate certain library use patterns of their teachers. Briefly stated, if the media center is an important agency to a teacher, either consciously or subconsciously, his students adopt a similar attitude.

Jay's dissertation in 1970[13] was designed to identify deterrents to the use of secondary school libraries and to use this information obtained by questionnaire from 88 teachers and 1,240 students to implement needed changes. Among other things that teachers reported needing were more time to plan classroom activity in a location where materials were available for examination and more consultative assistance in knowing what was available; interestingly enough, there emerged in this investigation the realization that also needed by teachers was the conviction that library use was necessary to teach their subject.

That the teacher's belief in the value of a media center is germane becomes apparent when one views the inability of researchers to determine with accuracy the composition of a library-oriented teacher based on certain quantifiable characteristics. Witness for example the apparent conflict between Donnelly[14] and Grassmeyer.[15] Donnelly, having determined that teachers in certain subject areas are more frequent users, further discloses that teachers with more experience and advanced degrees used the centers more often than other teachers. Grassmeyer, however, in his survey of 40 junior high school materials centers in 14 states contradicts this statement. He concluded that teachers utilizing the materials and services of the instructional materials center to the greatest extent were those with less than ten years of teaching experience and under 39 years of age.

This principle of conviction or commitment on the part of faculty members is supported by King[16] in his study of the relationship between teacher utilization of selected educational media and the level of sophistication of the educational media program. He found that in Oklahoma public schools educational media programs were more effective when the administration and faculty were committed to the provision and use of a wide variety of educational media and sources. Furthermore it was apparent that a positive relationship exists between well-established educational media programs and teacher utilization of educational media.

NEED FOR TEACHER TRAINING

It becomes obvious that much needs to be accomplished in making the teacher aware of the attributes of good media center service. Jay, Hall, and others refer to the lack of familiarity with library practice on the part of the teacher which certainly has contributed to any breach between the media center and the mainstream of the educational process. Tielke,[17] in his investigation of the relationship of selected environmental factors to the development of elementary school libraries, examined functional relationships among students, teachers, librarians, and others within the library. He concluded that classroom teachers have not realized the potential of the media center as an integrative force with classroom instructional programs. He goes further to state that the library program has been developed through the initiative of the librarian with little participation by teachers, principal, or other professional personnel.

The question then arises as to how to instill in the teacher the desire to utilize media center resources in his teaching. How is he to be imbued with the conviction and commitment which appear to be necessary characteristics of the effective media program in the schools? If the teacher really does have a definite role in the area of media center utilization by his students, it is part of his professional responsibility and therefore should have been part of his professional preparation. If this is not the case, then the teacher training institutions have been remiss.

In 1957, Cyphert[18] studied library use in the junior high schools of Pennsylvania with the view to understand among other things the working relationships of teachers and librarians. He found very little awareness on the part of the professionals involved and recommended that teacher training institutions give increased attention to the study of library services, materials, and utilization in both curriculum and methods courses. Donnelly recommended that such colleges should generally make a greater effort to acquaint prospective teachers with the value of the various instructional materials.[19] This was a virtual repeat of the recommendation made two years earlier by Hall[20] who urged that a concerted effort be made by colleges to orient prospective teachers to the multimedia approach to instruction.

Grassmeyer[21] found that such courses evidently do have merit since teachers who make use of materials and services indicated that courses and experiences in the use of the newer media acquired during their professional preparation were important factors. Like the others, he recommends continuation of teacher preparation programs and activities to facilitate the use of instructional materials and media for the improvement of instruction.

Happily this has come to pass and most teacher training institutions today include a course in media within the curriculum. Of course, increased awareness of the responsibility on the part of the teacher-training institution is a bit like closing the barn door after the horse has bolted, insofar as the practicing teacher is concerned. Since continuing education programs are only in the talking stages at many universities, part of the answer must lie in the development of good in-service training programs in the schools themselves. This was brought home forcibly by Jay[22] when she showed that the per capita average of book borrowing by the students increased after teachers had engaged in small group training programs.

The need was recognized earlier by Hall[23] in his concluding statement that in-service training for teachers is important so that they may make full use of the instructional media available for the teaching-learning process. Donnelly[24] reiterated these sentiments in his plea that the principal and the director of the instructional materials center acquaint all teachers with the personnel and services as well as the potential of the center.

Mehit[25] placed the responsibility back on the universities in his recommendation that library science departments should consider organizing local school library workshops so that teachers may better understand library science. Whatever the modus operandi, there appears to be a deplorable lack of such programs initiated by the schools, and whatever cooperative projects exist have arisen as a result of research studies undertaken by university personnel. Tielke[26] was dismayed by this condition of neglect and urged something be done about the absence of in-service work for teachers and librarians which emphasized extensive use of library resources.

Need for Instructional Planning and Design

An interesting example can be drawn from Jay's study[27] where one of the complaints registered by students was that teachers depended too much on the textbook alone, and there was no provision for use of outside materials. Barrilleaux[28] analyzed a similar situation by comparing the effects of instruction on the achievement and learning activities of students in eighth- and ninth-grade science classes with and without the use of a basic text. When student utilization of the center was observed, it was found that the group taught without the text visited the center more frequently, and devoted more time to library activities related to science classes, as well as more time to total library activities.

Of course, the vital element which is the real basis for relating library services to teacher utilization of materials must ultimately be the design of the curriculum. Neither teachers nor media specialists can shirk their responsibilities as architects of the learning process, and the new standards, *Media Programs: District and School*, acknowledge the importance of the issue. Awareness of the part of the teacher is most crucial to this comprehension of the need to work with all members of the educational team to establish short-term objectives and long-term goals and to implement policies designed to attain them. Since certain teaching methodologies require more media use and library participation than others, all members of the team should be knowledgeable in this regard.

In short, both teachers and media people should plan in a purposeful manner the implementation of educational activities designed to produce desirable outcomes or student behaviors. Hopefully, then, a teacher's conviction for the value of the media center arising out of knowledge gained either through education or experience translates into a willingness to work with the media specialist in implementing educational activities.

Importance of Media Centers

Let us assume for the sake of our discussion the need for teachers who favor extending their activities to include library-based media. We do know that it is desirable from an educational viewpoint to link the activities of teachers and media specialists. Studies conducted on student performance have pointed in a favorable way to the beneficial nature of the school library operation. Alongside the framework of instructional design to achieve specified objectives in education lies research in librarianship, which, although not shaped exclusively by that framework, does support the importance of the school library operation in fulfilling the educational goals of the school. Teachers working with media specialists do better than teachers working without them.

In his study of 188 sixth-grade students in 23 Oregon elementary schools, Gengler[29] compared students taught by teachers with those taught by teachers and librarians. He found that employment of qualified librarians, through instructional classes and individual aid, can substantially assist the classroom teacher in developing problem-solving abilities of elementary school children.

McMillen,[30] in 1965, examined the library programs in Ohio schools to determine among other things the degree of academic achievement of the pupils. His finding was that schools with good libraries and full-time librarians were superior to schools with minimal or no library service in the area of reading comprehension. Barrilleaux[31] found the library materials approach to compare favorably to the textbook approach in science achievement and ability to interpret science reading for certain groups of students.

Yarling[32] studied groups of youngsters as fourth graders and later as sixth graders in schools with and without a central library. He compared them in their mastery of certain skills and found that two of the reading skills, outlining and notetaking, were significantly improved in the experimental school. The implication was that these skills were strengthened by the library. The ability of students to express ideas effectively concerning their readings was also improved in significant fashion.

As would be expected, when mastery of library skills was examined as a desirable end in itself, the presence of a media center was a key factor. Yarling also reported that on a library skills test and library acquaintance test, students to whom the center had been accessible for three years performed significantly better. McMillen[33] supports this position in his find-

23

ing that students in schools with good library service were significantly better in the area of knowledge and use of reference materials than those with minimal or no library service.

CRITICAL ROLE OF THE MEDIA SPECIALIST

If learning activities include library-based media and if the library is accessible, is the media specialist important? As reported earlier in this chapter, Mehit[34] felt that the physical structure of the library was not enough to assure student use. Only one of the schools he studied had a full-time librarian, which led him to consider the central position of librarians. With scholarly caution, he recommended research on the effect of adding librarians.

In Bishop's study identifying the valuable learning experiences of nearly 400 fifth and sixth graders in Illinois,[35] one of the two critical elements in the library experience was the personality of the librarian. Not surprisingly, school librarians were perceived as the major source of help in using the library. Important to the students were their ability and willingness to help them locate materials, their efforts to teach efficient library usage, their methods of discipline, their efforts to inform them of the library's contents, and their interest in the personal needs of students.

Although the other and more important influential element in Bishop's study was the combination of materials and equipment, this element centered around availability, utility, and organization. These are characteristics which have marked the practice of librarianship since its inception in the days of antiquity. What the youngsters have identified in the successful media center experience is nothing more (nor nothing less) than professional performance on the part of the librarian.

Indeed, a dedicated media specialist will reach students not only by possession of personal warmth, but will seek to create access to materials and to develop services. Fortin,[36] in 1970, studied the life values and work satisfaction of school librarians in Wisconsin and found they are committed to the provision of appropriate library materials and services to students. They also wish to work with faculty to achieve school objectives. He felt that the impact of the library on the educational program rests with the librarian who is satisfied with his or her job, and recommended a broader study of school librarians' backgrounds, activities, personal attitudes, and satisfactions in order to attract candidates.

Development of job satisfaction. It is felt by most students of human behavior that job satisfaction develops from demonstrated ability to perform tasks which are considered to be significant and meaningful to the worker and to his colleagues and superiors. The commitment to provide services which characterized Fortin's librarians he found to be dependent to a great extent on such satisfaction with their jobs. There is much evidence to show that teachers consider the media specialist to be important (although they may not quite understand the nature of that importance). In the study conducted by the National Education Association, most teachers felt the library (librarian) to be a necessary element in the educational program.[37]

Lacock[38] found that teachers recognize the media specialist as an important and integral part of the instructional program. He showed that teachers and media specialists are in close agreement on tasks performed in connection with instructional design as well as consultation and utilization. Hall[39] described the importance of the staff of the materials center and indicated that teachers respond even more readily to services if the media director has had classroom teaching experience (which the great majority have had). He states flatly that administrators and teachers do approve of the instructional materials center in the implementation of the curriculum.

One can see that the media specialist needs a healthy measure of self-esteem which must necessarily arise from a feeling of self-confidence with respect to his or her competence. Educational background is of inestimable value here. Wert[40] showed that media specialists who received more extensive formal education were concerned with making libraries educationally more effective. She found that school librarians with larger amounts of formal education developed more extensive programs of reader services, and spent more time on such services. In addition, these services were used more frequently than were those offered by librarians with only undergraduate minors in library science. The resulting benefit was that students in schools with better educated librarians tended to use the library more to complete class assignments. This coincides with Fortin's finding that well-trained librarians found their satisfaction in a well-developed service program.[41]

Necessity of the Team Effort

The research described in the preceding pages has indicated the nature of the problem as it exists regarding full utilization of media center resources and services in the schools. Although teachers may consider the center to be important, there appears to be very little real contact with the media specialist. Unfortunately, teachers and media specialists alike seem to operate in a vacuum without recourse to the expertise available in their intellectual community. Tielke[42] has pointed out that library programs have developed independently of teachers while Cyphert[43] has shown that the librarian has not become involved in curriculum planning.

Fortunately, school personnel are becoming increasingly aware that this situation cannot be suffered to exist for much longer without real harm to the educational process. The age of technology is here and it brings with it new techniques of instruction and new informational approaches based on new developments in the field of learning theory. Neither the teacher nor the media specialist can afford the luxury of isolation if either is to remain atop or even abreast of developments in this dynamic period. Reason and logic tell us that all changes cannot be beneficial in all respects, but the same logic would indicate that we had better know why. Without this awareness neither the professional librarian nor the teacher is in any position to help preserve that which is good and forestall the implementation of that which is not.

Obviously, the armchair speculators reported in chapter 1 have a valid point to make. The plea for cooperation is one which must not go unheeded. As was pointed out, however, the utility of these opinion articles for practicing professionals is rather limited. They do not clarify the roles of teachers and media specialists as part of the educational process, since there is no indication of the degree of influence which may be exerted on the student in the effort to make him a library user. Existing research comes closer to this enlightenment, but even so, there still exists a murky grey area which must be penetrated. This book hopes to provide a framework or springboard for further understanding.

Obviously, both teachers and media specialists are indispensable to the functioning of an efficient school media center program. The question of influence on student use, however, is the key element underlying the present study. The original effort was predicated on the belief that the role of the teacher is the consideration of primary importance, the teacher being the goal setter, evaluator, and ultimate authority in the student's academic career. As such, he or she enjoys a unique position in bearing the greatest responsibility for that which the student wishes to achieve. Too often, in the author's opinion, what this amounts to is, pure and simple, a grade, without the concomitant knowledge. An effort has been made in this study to completely neutralize the student's desire for the grade as motivation.

If it is true that the teacher can influence his or her charges in the manner in which we believe he can, the ramifications are quite clear. The existing literature indicates that certain teachers are generally unaware of the value of a media center in the implementation of their teaching objectives. Therefore, it is small wonder that students do not become habitual media center and library users if those who exercise the greatest authority and are closest to them in the intellectual environment generally are not cognizant of the educative potential of this resource. The naiveté of the teacher is reflected in the lack of concern by the students. This, then, is the key to student use. Frequent library or media center utilization by the teacher is the major ingredient.

It is in this respect that one is able to perceive the importance of the media specialist. Obviously, he or she has neither the constant close contact with students nor the primary responsibility for their academic careers. In short, the media specialist's hold on or capability for influencing the student is much less than that of his or her colleague in the classroom. Too often the media professional is complacent in his or her understanding of this condition and is merely occupied with making the library a pleasant place to visit, one which will retain if not create library users.

The opinion of this researcher has always been that the foregoing is not enough to justify the school media specialist's professional existence. Certainly, a pleasant atmosphere, relatively free from tension and worry, staffed by an interested, personable professional is important. This brings to mind, however, a picture of so many of those who have preceded us: gracious, friendly, charming types who welcomed all who desired to make use of the library's services. As comfortable as the picture appears to be, today's media specialist must be more of an activist than the genteel creature of yesteryear ever imagined.

Understanding the Media Specialist-Teacher Relationship

It is true that the major focal point of this book is the teacher's role. We feel that the teacher's frequency and depth of contact with the student cannot be matched by the media specialist. It is also true, however, that if the media professional is only a secondary influence on the student, he or she is assuredly the primary bibliographic referent of the teacher. In effect, the media specialist influences the influencer and cannot be relegated to a position of superficial nature as relates to the process of student use. To better understand the nature of the relationship is an important undertaking.

Recalling the model of teacher-student-media center interaction presented in chapter 1 may help to place the research in proper perspective. Each of the six steps or components of the interface have been studied in ways of which the previously mentioned studies are representative. El-Hagrasy examined the teacher's library background and experience (step 1), and Sister Peter Claver the teacher's attitudes (step 2). The National Education Association research project, in a comprehensive but loose manner, encompasses both of these and included the teacher's participation in center activities (step 3), while Knapp, among other things, dealt with the teacher's utilization of library resources (step 4). Hostrop and Jay reported on the teacher's influence as measured by student use of books (step 5), while student benefits derived from library use (step 6) were examined by McMillen and Yarling.

Most of the previous research has been of a descriptive nature and has been constrained thereby. The natural limitations of the descriptive method are such that, although an awareness and insight are provided into the situation as it exists, little can be uncovered regarding causes. These studies also tend to rely upon teacher's estimates and reports of their own characteristics (background, attitudes, participation, utilization) as recorded by questionnaire or interview responses. Invariably, they deal with assignments of required materials in assessing utilization.

The original study upon which this book is based used as a focal point steps 4 and 5 in an examination of teacher influence on student use. In this fashion, we had concerned ourselves with the level of media center involvement in the instructional process. Fundamental in this respect are the questions posed by Knapp, as previously noted in chapter 1:

1. What is the extent of the contribution to course work?
2. What is the nature of the contribution to the instructional program?
3. What factors limit the contribution to the instructional program?
4. What should be the contribution to the instructional program?

What About the Administrator?

Although the role of the administrator is not the subject of direct concern in this book, the author would be remiss if he were not to devote some space to its representation. The role of the administrator is an important one, for in essence all that can be implemented with respect to the improvement of library operations must have approval and support of the chief authority. Past research efforts have recognized the vital nature of the administrative responsibility in the creation and development of good media programs.

Sister Peter Claver was dismayed at what she referred to as the lack of leadership at higher levels of administration in providing the necessary motivation to use the school library as a resource center in the teaching program.[44] This was similar to Tielke's disclosure that there was little participation by the principal (or teachers) in the development of library programs.[45]

Cyphert[46] urged that principals provide channels of communication between teachers and media specialists to match needs with resources. As head of the school, the principal should see that media people spend a greater proportion of their time in curriculum study. A real assessment of the place of the media center in facilitating superior instruction should be undertaken under his direction with the involvement of the faculty. Mehit[47] in similar fashion refers to the need for administrators in cooperation with the teachers to establish written library policies for their schools.

Jay[48] reported the need for conviction on the part of teachers that library usage was necessary to teach their subject. This conviction was supplied by what she termed a re-emphasis by principals of the role of the school library in daily teaching, by establishing small group sessions which eventually led to increased student borrowing. As reported previously, Donnelly[49] also urged establishment of in-service sessions under the leadership of the principal to acquaint all teachers with the personnel and services of the instructional materials center.

The important responsibility of the administrator in bringing concerned professionals together cannot be gainsaid and certainly should not be overlooked in creating efficient media programs. In the effective administrator lies the capability to promulgate desirable and innovative policies through the proper exercise of his authority. The "exercise in propriety" can be accomplished only if that person is enlightened as to the nature of a good media center. The cooperative venture, then, in reality involves a tripartite of professional responsibilities which must be known and understood in order to achieve success.

Notes

1. Patricia B. Knapp, "Role of the Library of a Given College in Implementing the Course and Non-Course Objectives of the College," (Unpublished Ph.D. dissertation, Univ. of Chicago, 1957).

2. _____, _College Teaching and the College Library_. (ACRL Monograph no. 23 [Chicago: American Library Assn., 1959]).

3. Sister Mary Peter Claver Ducat, O.P., "Student and Faculty Use of the Library in Three Secondary Schools" (Unpublished Ph.D. dissertation, Columbia Univ., 1960).

4. George Mehit, "Effects of Type of Library Service Upon Utilization of Books by Sixth Grade Pupils in Selected County Elementary Schools of Northeastern Ohio" (Unpublished Ed.D. dissertation, Western Reserve Univ., 1965).

5. Robert James Graham, "The Impact of Title II of the Elementary and Secondary Education Act of 1965 on Selected Michigan High Schools" (Unpublished Ed.D. dissertation, Univ. of Michigan, 1969).

6. Howard Clayton, "An Investigation of Various Social and Economic Factors Influencing Student Use of One College Library" (Unpublished Ph.D. dissertation, Univ. of Oklahoma, 1965).

7. William Woods, "Factors Influencing Student Library Use: An Analysis of Studies" (Unpublished master's thesis, Univ. of Chicago, 1965).

8. Richard Hostrop, "The Relationship of Academic Success and Selected Other Factors to Student Use of Library Materials at College of the Desert" (Unpublished Ed.D. dissertation, Univ. of California at Los Angeles, 1966).

9. Woods, "Factors Influencing Student Library Use."

10. National Education Assn. Research Div. *The Secondary School Teacher and Library Services* (Research monograph 1958—M1; Washington, DC: The Association, 1958).

11. Edward Joseph Donnelly, "The Organization and Administration of Instructional Materials Centers in Selected High Schools" (Unpublished Ed.D. dissertation, Univ. of Nebraska, 1965).

12. Saad Mohammed el-Hagrasy, "The Teacher's Role in Library Service" (Unpublished Ph.D. dissertation, Rutgers Univ., 1961).

13. Hilda Lease Jay, "Increasing the Use of Secondary School Libraries as a Teaching Tool" (Unpublished Ed.D. dissertation, New York Univ., 1970).

14. Donnelly, "Instructional Materials Centers."

15. Donald Leroy Grassmeyer, "The Organization and Administration of Instructional Materials Centers in Selected Junior High Schools" (Univ. of Nebraska, 1966).

16. Kenneth Lee King, "An Evaluation of Teacher Utilization of Selected Educational Media in Relation to the Level of Sophistication of the Educational Media Program in Selected Oklahoma Public Schools" (Unpublished Ed.D. dissertation, Univ. of Oklahoma, 1969).

17. Elton Fritz Tielke, "A Study of the Relationship of Selected Environmental Factors to the Development of Elementary School Libraries" (Unpublished Ed.D. dissertation, Univ. of Texas, 1968).

18. Frederick R. Cyphert, "Current Practice in the Use of the Library in Selected Junior High Schools in Pennsylvania" (Unpublished Ed.D. dissertation, Univ. of Pittsburgh, 1957).

19. Donnelly, "Instructional Media Centers."

20. Sedley Duane Hall, "A Comparative Study of Two Types of Organization of Instructional Materials Centers" (Univ. of Nebraska Teachers College, 1963).

21. Grassmeyer, "Organization and Administration."

22. Jay, "Secondary School Libraries as a Teaching Tool."

23. Hall, "A Comparative Study."

24. Donnelly, "Instructional Media Centers."

25. Mehit, "Utilization of Books by Sixth Grade Pupils."

26. Tielke, "Relationship of Selected Environmental Factors."

27. Jay, "Secondary School Libraries as a Teaching Tool."

28. Louis E. Barrilleaux, "An Experimental Investigation of the Effects of Multiple Library Sources as Compared to the Use of a Basic Textbook on Student Achievement and Learning Activity in Junior High School Science" (Unpublished Ph.D. dissertation, Univ. of Iowa, 1965).

29. Charles Richard Gengler, "A Study of Selected Problem Solving Skills Comparing Teacher Instructed Students with Librarian-Teacher Instructed Students" (Unpublished Ed.D. dissertation, Univ. of Oregon, 1965).

30. Ralph Donnelly McMillen, "An Analysis of Library Programs and a Determination of the Educational Justification of These Programs in Selected Elementary Schools of Ohio" (Unpublished Ed.D. dissertation, Western Reserve Univ., 1965).

31. Barrilleaux, "An Experimental Investigation."

32. James Robert Yarling, "Children's Understandings and Use of Selected Library-Related Skills in Two Elementary Schools, One with and One without a Centralized Library" (Unpublished Ed.D. dissertation, Ball State Univ., 1968).

33. McMillen, "An Analysis of Library Programs."

34. Mehit, "Utilization of Books by Sixth Grade Pupils."

35. Martha Dell Bishop, "Identification of Valuable Learning Experiences in Centralized Elementary School Libraries" (Unpublished Ed.D. dissertation, George Peabody College for Teachers, 1963).

36. Clifford Charles Fortin, "The Relation of Certain Personal and Environmental Characteristics of School Librarians to Their Life Values and Work Satisfactions" (Unpublished Ph.D. dissertation, Univ. of Minnesota, 1970).

37. National Education Assn., *The Secondary School Teacher and Library Services.*

38. Donald Wayne Lacock, "The Media Specialist and Tasks Related to the Design, Production and Utilization of Instructional Materials" (Unpublished Ed.D. dissertation, Univ. of Nebraska, 1971).

39. Hall, "A Comparative Study."

40. Lucille Mathena Wert, "Library Education and High School Library Services" (Unpublished Ph.D. dissertation, Univ. of Illinois, 1970).

41. Fortin, "Personal and Environmental Characteristics of School Librarians."

42. Tielke, "Relationship of Selected Environmental Factors."

43. Cyphert, "Current Practice in the Use of the Library."

44. Sister Mary Peter Claver Ducat, "Student and Faculty Use of the Library."

45. Tielke, "Relationship of Selected Environmental Factors."

46. Cyphert, "Current Practice in the Use of the Library."

47. Mehit, "Utilization of Books by Sixth Grade Pupils."

48. Jay, "Secondary School Libraries as a Teaching Tool."

49. Donnelly, "Instructional Materials Centers."

3

Structure and Development of the Study

Because this study seeks to isolate the influences leading to students' media center use, an integral part of this effort must be to identify the qualities of a successful teacher. It is incumbent, therefore, that we closely examine the available studies of teacher effectiveness to ascertain from the literature which qualities are deemed significant in this regard. Also necessary to the study is the literature pertaining to the relationship of supplementary materials (library/media center resources) to the learning process. Finally, there is the literature which deals with the role of the media center in the implementation of the mathematics curriculum, an area directly related to our inquiry. We begin then by surveying these three areas of concern in order to establish the effort in its proper context and to provide a viable framework for our purposes.

Once the necessary background material has been examined, part II of this chapter will unfold in a natural manner for the reader. The plan of the study is revealed and the steps taken by the researcher are described, as is his choice of instruments. In providing this awareness or perspective, this section of the book merits the special attention of the prospective researcher as well as the individual who seeks enlightenment about the manner in which research problems are envisioned and developed. Of course, in the interests of economy much analytical material, including numerous tables, has been deleted. The serious researcher may wish to refer to the original study[1] for a more detailed description.

I. Related Literature

The Literature of Teacher Influence

Prior to finding out to what extent a teacher can help to create student users of nonrequired library materials, we are faced with the awesome task of identifying the components of teacher influence when divorced from one of the natural weapons in the teacher's arsenal, that is the administration of the grade itself. Obviously, the major power bases from which teacher influence is derived lie notably within the realms of either threat of punishment or promise of reward.

One of the very unique features of this effort, however, as opposed to the studies of the past is its consequent removal of these two bases of power in its sharp focus on nonrequired materials rather than mandatory assignments. Here, then, the real influence of a teacher (or any individual for that matter), devoid of the trappings manifested by the type of situation in which it is contrived, is exposed for what it is; that is to say, any teacher is influential by virtue of his position as teacher. However, if the reward-punishment basis is the sole source of influence, the effect lasts only as long as the teacher controls the students' grades. We all remember occasions in our academic careers when the teachers bored us to tears and "turned us off" as human beings or, worse yet, made no impression at all. If there were assigned readings in such circumstances, they were undertaken only as a defense mechanism against a poor grade. As a consequence, the library experiences themselves were flat and unrewarding and ceased to exist once the courses had terminated and become part of our nebulous, better forgotten past history.

Obviously, such teachers were not influential in the manner that we require. We are seeking to identify the truly influential person who just happens to be a teacher. We are interested in such identification because of our profound belief that within this person's capability lies the key to student library use at a higher level of involvement and longevity. This may well be the first step in the creation of the now legendary lifelong user of the public library.

QUALITIES OF INFLUENCE OR EFFECTIVENESS— PERSONALITY AND EXPERTISE

In chapter 1 consideration was given to the complexity of the phenomenon associated with causality in this study. What influence or effectiveness a teacher possesses in his everyday contact with his pupils, although quite important to the learning situation, is difficult to analyze. Especially is this true in dealing with a teacher's suggestion as opposed to a teacher's assignment. This study proceeded on the assumption, as have many in the past, that pupil reaction or response is as much or more a function of the teaching mystique as it is a characteristic of the pupil.

The analysis of teacher characteristics has been a common and familiar research area to those who would examine the learning situation, and as a result many efforts have been undertaken. It is fortunate that this rather

33

extensive body of literature has itself received a great deal of attention. Studies of teacher behavior, effectiveness, competence, or influence as it is here described have been reported at length, and several surveys of this literature have been completed.

As is true of most research concerning topics in the social sciences, there is a great deal of controversy surrounding the results and findings. Hagrasy[2] provides awareness of this, having reviewed the literature of teacher behavior since the turn of the century and indicating his reliance upon the surveys of existing studies. His conclusions reached after a thorough examination of such surveys as those by Barr[3] and Domas and Tiedman,[4] are that the aspects of teacher behavior which have been studied are numerous and include almost all possible predictions of teacher effectiveness while the same is true of the criteria by which that behavior is measured.

Amid the controversy, however, one trait is clearly revealed as an important teacher characteristic in the opinion of students. In students' assessment of a teacher's impact, the factor of desirable personality ranks highly in a majority of the studies surveyed. Because of this it merits our representation in the hypothesis (*see* p. 7) as one of the two major factors in the assessment of teacher influence.

The other factor relates to the expertise of the teacher. Although not nearly as clear-cut a choice as was the personality factor, there is an ample body of literature which recognizes its value. For our purposes, it may be especially valid an indicator since our study involves competitive youngsters of above average ability. It is not unlikely that the respect and admiration accorded the subject expert by these pupils is as great as that accorded the desired personality (especially with respect to class-related voluntary effort such as the reading of nonrequired library materials).

The use of a measurable effect on student behavior as a criterion of effectiveness or influence is another strong point of the study. As long ago as 1913 Davidson[5] described the efficiency of the teacher as lying essentially in the effects produced upon the pupils. Today, with the emphasis on measurable objectives the tenet is no less valid. How to measure such effectiveness has always been a problem. Here, we propose to alter the reading patterns of students, ascribing such changes to the inducement of a teacher recognized as influential by virtue of his personality, his expertise, or both.

Therefore, the two characteristics are taken together as predictors of the teacher's influence with pupils, and no effort is made to separate the two in terms of the effects on pupils' activity. Regarding this dual representation is Freehill's expression that "The quality of teaching beyond the crucial minimum of failure is related to ability, college entrance test scores, and academic success. It is at least as closely related to records of social participation and attitude."[6] In the following pages the reader will learn of past research efforts and how these relate to the present study.

PREEMINENCE OF PERSONALITY

The oldest study to represent personality as the key factor in the character of a teacher was that by Bird in 1917.[7] Using the estimates of 150 girls attending normal school, 139 high school girls, and 253 high school boys as to what teacher traits were most important, Bird found that kindness received highest frequency of mention, about 79 percent. Following kindness the traits most often mentioned were fairness (51%), sense of humor (38%), and discipline (37%), although there were some small differences in the responses between groups of students.

A quarter-century later, this finding was supported by an analysis of teacher efficiency rating scales identifying personality to be a vital factor in teaching success.[8] In a survey conducted of 1,588 high school students who responded by questionnaire to the rating of 78 teachers, the six characteristics found to be most important were: (1) helpfulness, (2) friendliness, (3) kindness, (4) good disposition, (5) sense of humor, and (6) fairness.[9]

Of great help was the report of the Harvard Teacher Education Research Project conducted in the early fifties. It comprises eight studies on teacher behavior out of which emerged four doctoral dissertations.[10] The most important to this work was the one by Cogan since it dealt with behaviors of three varieties and also considered the phenomenon of self-initiated work as well as required assignments.[11] This effort proved to be the greatest single boon to the author in terms of the conceptual development of his study.

Cogan investigated the relationships between teacher behaviors and the amounts of both required and class-related, self-initiated work performed by pupils. He surveyed 987 junior high school pupils and 33 teachers, the latter group being scored by the former on three different scales. This provided data out of which came three important measures: (1) a measure of the extent to which a teacher is friendly and warm (inclusive behavior); (2) a measure of dominative, aggressive, rejectant, preclusive behavior; and (3) a measure of the extent of technical competence which included skillful classroom management and command of the subject matter (conjunctive behavior).

Cogan's primary emphasis on the reports of pupils as a source of data is an important feature of his work, as it is in ours, since the rating of the teacher by the pupils is an absolute necessity. In a later article Cogan explains that the pupils are in an excellent position to report on teacher behaviors and their own work. "The behavior of teachers as perceived by the pupils influences the nature and extent of (1) the motivation of pupils, (2) communication with pupils, and (3) the 'tone' of the classroom."[12]

It was Cogan's finding that only the inclusive variable demonstrated a pronounced relationship to the amount of self-initiated work on the part of the pupil which led this researcher to the design of the present investigation to determine why some teachers are more influential than others. He offered three possible explanations for the evidence, the first of which concerns identification. Self-initiated work was viewed as an index of similarity of teacher-pupil values. Since the major stimulus for self-initiated work comes from the pupil rather than the teacher, the pupil has accepted these teacher values as his own. The second interpretation emphasized the importance of the teacher-pupil relationship and stated that the child by doing his work brings himself into symbolic proximity to the teacher. If this is a pleasant association, it is furthered by doing things that the teacher would like. Thirdly, the amount of self-initiated work was viewed as an index of the pupils' interest in the subject.[13]

In examining the three interpretations, it is evident that the pupil's reaction to the teacher is an important consideration in each case. In fact, the warmth of the teacher-pupil relationship is a prerequisite in both the first and second interpretations, and in the third instance it is recognized that aspects of the teacher-pupil relationship affect the pupil's interest in a subject. Findings such as these reaffirmed the conviction of the investigator that teacher influence in the present study may be examined in profitable fashion by determining the pupils' feelings for the teacher.

Five years later, Medley and Mitzel[14] reviewed several studies involving teacher ratings in an attempt to determine what relationship existed between such ratings and the amount of pupil learning in the classroom. Pupil learning was not related to ratings of the teacher, but of importance is the fact that the only significant relationship was between these ratings and what was termed the "emotional climate" of the classroom. Thus the element of success was judged by those in authority to reflect certain desirable personality traits.

How a pupil perceives and reacts to the teacher's feelings for him must necessarily be an important consideration, since the more positive the children's perception of their teachers' feelings, the better their academic achievement and the more desirable their classroom behavior as rated by their teachers.[15] Therefore, a teacher who is positive and receptive in nature is capable of exercising influence over students. Indeed, personality has been judged to be the best predictor of teaching success.[16]

In 1964 Salomon, Bezdek, and Rosenberg reviewed the literature of teacher behavior studies and reported that most behavior studies are set up to emphasize either of two teacher behaviors: inclusive, or integrative, behavior, characterized by instructor warmth, a student-centered atmosphere, and an emphasis on student participation; or preclusive, or dominative, behavior which reflects instructor determination of goals and emphasizes the lecture method.[17] Previous studies associated with pupils' learning were categorized on this basis and identified either the presence or absence of relationships with such teacher behaviors. As we might expect in line with our reasoning, several studies (Flanders,[18] Faw,[19] and Amidon and Flanders[20]) pointed to the favorable nature of inclusive behavior. Replogle in his 1968 dissertation demonstrated that a relationship exists in mathematics instruction between teacher-pupil similarities and (1) pupil grades, and (2) compatibility of the teacher-pupil relationship as perceived by both teachers and pupils.[21]

IMPORTANCE OF TEACHER EXPERTISE

We have already alluded to the element of expertise as probably being of secondary importance to personality within the framework of teacher influence. When taken together, however, we feel that the emergence of an influential figure can be predicted with a high degree of accuracy. Indeed, it is exceedingly difficult to separate the two. Sanderson and Anderson[22] in a 1960 study suggested that teachers judged to be inspirational by their students are more effective in imparting academic facts and concepts to their students than teachers not so judged by their students in the field of mathematics. Certainly, here is a gray area involving a mix of personality and expertise. The remainder of the studies when indicating the importance of expertise also did so in tandem with the factor of personality.

Most of the studies in this category date from the nineteen-forties, the earliest being that by Bousfield[23] who used 568 undergraduates in a two-part study to determine the qualities deemed by them to be important in the make-up of the college professor. The characteristics found to be statistically significant in order of frequency were: (1) interest in students, (2) fairness, (3) pleasing personality, (4) humor, and (5) mastery of subject. Another study had over 200 college students list the good qualities of teachers; the data was then tabulated for a total ranking. Of primary importance were: (1) knowledge of subject matter; (2) personality to put the course across; and (3) fairness.[24]

Barr[25] produced another valuable bibliography in 1961, a critical overview of 70 doctoral dissertations in the area of teacher effectiveness completed at the University of Wisconsin. In his introductory statement, he cites four criteria used to judge effectiveness in the past: (1) personal qualities, (2) competencies or skill, (3) pupil growth or effects of teaching, and (4) behavior control.

Of interest is Barr's reference to Peronto's 1942 dissertation[26] in which the latter found that in past studies only the knowledge of the subject matter and of the pupils as well as professional knowledge can be definitely established as discriminating between good and poor teachers. Knowledge of the pupils was considered to be an absence of discipline problems, ample opportunity for expression by students, and provision for individual differences. Interest and proficiency in the teacher-pupil relationship appeared to be related to the personal growth of pupils but unrelated to academic achievement.

A later analysis[27] of the abilities of 85 teachers, found two factors to be most directly related to the criterion of pupil achievement: (1) general knowledge; and (2) emotional adjustment of teachers. Found not to be important were a eulogizing attitude toward the teaching profession and the teacher rating scale factor. As we might expect, the emotional adjustment factor is related to personality, and therefore our case for causal relationships receives added support.

A final study was completed by Punke,[28] who stated that for most high school students teachers constitute the major school influence. In his examination of certain pupil-teacher relationships for 804 Alabama high school seniors he found no great differences between boys and girls in judging the qualities of the best and poorest teachers. There appeared to be a close interweaving between (1) knowledge and ability to explain subject matter; (2) interest, friendliness, and a pleasing personality; and (3) good discipline and fairness as qualities of good teachers.

Important to us is the interpretation Punke gives to teacher effectiveness. "It is of interest that, in the thinking of the 804 seniors studied, a teacher's understanding and getting along with students may be more closely related to his ability to explain subject matter and maintain discipline than has been implied by some writers on guidance or on education for social adjustment."[29]

Punke looked also at the school library and found no important sex differences concerning its use. Over half the students, both boys and girls, spend less than half an hour per day there. He suggested that factors which influence the amount of time spent in the library by the students are size of the library, usefulness, library practices, class schedules, curriculum practices, and teaching methods.[30]

INCONCLUSIVE RESULTS

The remainder of the studies of teacher effectiveness reported findings of no particular significance. That is, the characteristics of teachers these examined were not found to be related to anticipated pupil gains. The two earliest are 1945 efforts which relate to pupil growth and achievement.

Brookover[31] obtained pupil reactions to the teacher by asking eleven questions:

1. Is this teacher friendly to you?
2. Does this teacher join in your recreation?
3. Do you like to have this teacher join in your recreation?
4. Do you confide in this teacher?
5. Do you think this teacher is fair?
6. Do you admire this teacher personally?
7. Do you think this teacher is a sissy?
8. Do you think this teacher is good-looking?
9. Do you respect this teacher for academic ability?
10. Do you think this teacher is peculiar?
11. How long have you known this teacher?

He then attempted to relate these responses to gains in history information but could find no real association and only vague indications of relationships.

Gotham[32] employed three personality tests, three standardized teacher rating scales, and two unstandardized personality rating scales in a study involving 47 teachers and 338 pupils. He found that no significant relationship existed between the criterion of pupil change and the three personality test scores; no significant relationship was present between pupil change and various personal traits measured by the Rudisill Scale of Measurement of Personality of Elementary School Teachers; and only a small relationship existed between pupil change and the three teacher rating scales. In addition, efforts by Johnson,[33] Krumboltz,[34] Wispe,[35] and McKeachie[36] saw teacher behavior as making no difference to the learning situation.

Obviously there is a real lack of consensus among educators as to what constitutes real competency or effectiveness in teaching. Criteria measuring pupil growth are diverse in nature (social adjustment, motivation for learning, and knowledge gain) and meaningful relationships depend upon the standard employed. The important thing to us is that the inconclusive studies all used knowledge gain as the criterion; while in those studies which focused on motivation, *personality* and *expertise*, indeed, were judged to be important. Since *motivation* is the desired effect of the present study in our endeavor to create willing library users, the factors of personality and expertise are clearly integral to its development.

The Literature of Supplementary Materials

Another key feature of this study is the nature of the materials employed. Use is to be voluntary rather than mandated, and film material, books, and periodical articles all are to be included. This raises certain pedagogical issues. We have identified two categories to be treated: the multimedia approach and the place of the textbook. They are important to the successful design and conduct of this particular effort and should add considerably to the study's usefulness. Media specialists, teachers, and administrators ought to view supplementary materials in a similar rather than disparate manner, sharing certain understandings of their importance and potential.

The Media Center and the Multimedia Approach in Education

For over a decade, educators have been concerned with the structure of the learning process as described by Bruner in his influential and provocative work, *The Process of Education*.[37] Concept formation, sequential learning, and individualization have become familiar and widely promulgated topics in modern educational theory. The proponents of this theory emphasize the media of instruction and recommend that a diversity of media be employed.

Modern theorists refer to sensory experiences as pathways through which knowledge is received and the cross-media approach as a means of supplying these experiences. This approach, therefore, is recognized as "just good teaching."[38] Although there are dissenters who feel that the multimedia approach may not be as effective as single channel presentation,[39] they represent a small minority.

Naturally, these beliefs, when represented as philosophy and implemented as policy, greatly affect the composition and organization of the school media center. As important developments, they are given ample treatment in the literature providing us with analytical descriptions of the development of the school library as an instructional materials center, identifying the increased emphasis on intellectual excellence, individual differences, curriculum change, and methodology.[40] Similar is the treatment accorded the advent of instructional materials on the educational scene.[41] Much publicity was given to the decision of the American Association of School Librarians to accept the IMC philosophy as being in keeping with modern educational thought and a logical extension of instructional responsibilities.[42]

Typical fare for the 1960s were the descriptions of individual multimedia centers, their establishment, maintenance, and operation,[43] and reports of increased use of school libraries because of efforts put forth by teachers to increase individualization of instruction and assignments designed to require independent study and research.[44] Nor has the current emphasis on innovation in education been neglected with respect to the importance of providing materials in adequate quantity as well as quality. The changing needs of students and faculty members serve to identify the media center as a key in free inquiry and as the laboratory for implementation of the problem-solving approach. Quite correctly we have recognized its value in providing basic instructional materials for the achievement of some curriculum objectives and supplementary materials for the achievement of others.[45] The predominant feeling today points to a broadening of the concept of instructional materials and thus the concept of the school library itself has grown to embrace all conceivable materials of communication. We are quite certain that not every child has to read the same book,[46] and that books alone will not provide children with a total learning experience. Thus, the multimedia approach has given us our present-day media center.

That the multimedia approach has been recognized by those in authority as a valid educational premise and one which affects the library is best demonstrated in terms of the financial support which has been received, making possible the great growth period of the 1960s. In its first year of operation, 1965-1966, Title II of the Elementary and Secondary Education Act reached almost 90 percent of the school children in the United States, and about 19 percent of the materials were audiovisual in nature.[47] Subsequent years produced increased allocations and, equally important, the development of government-sponsored institutes on multimedia.[48]

Therefore, we feel we would have been remiss had we decided not to include audiovisual materials in the present investigation, examining their distinctive effects, if any, on the willingness or enthusiasm of the youngsters in undertaking extra or nonrequired work. This feature adds another important dimension to our effort, since it is of great value to both teachers and media specialists.

PLACE OF THE TEXTBOOK

With the emphasis today on individualized study, the textbook has become a controversial issue largely due to its confining nature.[49] Certainly, in any consideration of the nature and value of supplementary materials in education, it would be inconceivable to omit reference to the position of the textbook. Even with the present emphasis on the variety of instructional materials and the advantages in their use, the textbook is still the chief tool of the teacher in the implementation of the curriculum. This is not only true of mathematics but is characteristic of most subjects offered in the general college preparatory curriculum.

Therefore, a natural outgrowth of the consideration of the multimedia approach is an examination of present educational theory with respect to the role of the textbook in the learning process. Since the present study deals with nonrequired materials among which are several titles from textbook series (included in the bibliographies for pupils), it is important to comprehend the sentiments of educational planners and practitioners.

The best survey of research in this area, which appeared over a decade ago, turned up several pertinent references.[50] Conflicting results emerged from two studies dealing with mathematics texts. Bhargava,[51] analyzing the scope and sequence of computational programs in seven arithmetic series ranging from grades three to six, found differences in scope but general agreement on the sequence of steps. Mauro,[52] in contrast, found less agreement in the area of sequence than in grade placement for ten series of mathematics texts, although the greatest difference concerned methods of introducing subskills. Two studies concerned with social studies texts for the middle grades are worth considering, since they compare the multiple text approach to that of the single text. Causey[53] found greater competency in work-study skills as well as greater progress through the diversified rather than the single text at the third and sixth grade levels. Schneider[54] found little difference in subject matter knowledge attainment and behavior improvement among fourth graders, but felt that the multiple text approach held more merit and potential in the area of work-study skills.

Inconsistency in research results regarding the use of textbooks is only a small indication of the nature of the controversy within the profession. Since Bruner's work has gained ascendancy, it has become more professionally correct to criticize use of the textbook as the only source of information, and the great majority of the writings reflect this philosophy. Supplementary reading, therefore, takes on added importance and has been promulgated in the literature as sound educational practice; it is certainly a requirement of any teacher who seeks to make the classroom textbook more functional.[55] Not uncommon, then, is the reference to the "tyrannical narrowness" of the era of the single textbook and its welcome demise.[56]

The text, however, has not been without its defenders,[57] although they are relatively few in number and offer what may be termed "qualified support." Those who defend the textbook from what may be undue criticism hasten to point out that it is only one of many sources and proceed to encourage as much outside reading as is possible from as many sources as is possible.[58] The textbook, in truth, is a valuable resource only to the intelligent and creative teacher who realizes its limitations[59] and makes an effort to implement a multiple text approach within his teaching methodology.[60]

Clearly, there has been an abundance of articles in the literature of education over the past decade and a half which examine the unfavorable position of those who would limit teaching to a single textbook. These efforts are quite diverse in nature. There is the scathing indictment of the straight textbook provided by the scholarly and influential Bruner who states that "the expository account with a solely descriptive aim may produce a chronic somnambulism where its own subject is concerned."[61] In contrast there is the simple expression from a state school superintendent, "The single textbook is generally inadequate as a curriculum guide, as a course of study, or as the single media [sic] for effective learning."[62]

Such writings are representative of the feelings of the profession at this time and should indicate the very strong desire to provide good teaching by a careful and well-structured use of materials of varied nature and form. This may be an obvious consideration for subjects which rely heavily upon verbal communication, since it is quite clear that the distinction between textbook and trade book or library book is becoming more difficult to make.[63] Mathematics teachers may be more reluctant, however, and rightly may ask what advantage accrues to them in using supplementary materials. This book was written to answer that question.

The Literature of Mathematics and the Media Center

In choosing mathematics as the subject to be examined in this study, there is one additional consideration. Unlike the other subjects, mathematics as an area of library concern has not attracted a great deal of attention in the past. Research efforts have been extremely rare. Burns and Dessart's survey of research in secondary school mathematics provided no citations related to the library role.[64]

One of the rare investigations, already cited in chapter 2 with respect to the importance of the teacher's role, is the 1958 study by the National Education Association. This study greatly aids our understanding of the existing situation. Mathematics, industrial arts, and business education classes were considered to be minor users of the library. Teachers in these subjects tended to feel little responsibility for making the development of library skills a part of the content of their curriculum and made little effort to motivate pupils in library use.[65]

Since teachers of mathematics generally consider library media to be relatively unimportant to the effective teaching of their subject, it is not difficult to understand the lack of interest in the interface between the media center and mathematics instruction. This lack of interest is characteristic of both parties, media specialists and mathematics teachers, and may serve to produce a situation in which the lack of enthusiasm results from the interaction of limited demand upon limited services available.[66]

To be sure, we recognize the distinctive quality of mathematics in its dependence on skills, techniques, and operations which may serve in part to explain the unwillingness to indulge reading-oriented supplemental approaches. Even Cogan found in his study of teacher behavior that productive behaviors didn't hold up as well for mathematics as they did in science. Mathematics productivity did, however, relate to teacher behavior in a manner comparable to English, especially with regard to self-initiated work.[67]

We do feel, therefore, that our examination of the relationships between mathematics instruction and the media center is a worthwhile endeavor, and one which is needed to gain more insight into an important topic. The survey of the literature provides us with two broad general categories; writings which support the media center's role, and writings which do not.

The Minor Role of the Media Center in Mathematics Instruction

Unfortunately, like the National Education Association study, all three remaining research efforts have indicated the media center to be a minor consideration in the teaching of mathematics. Nietling,[68] in his study of the use of the problem approach at the college level, made little mention of the library. He failed to point up any difference in attitude, interest, or morale between groups taught by the problem approach or by the traditional method. There was some evidence to suggest that students in the experimental group devoted more time to mathematics study and may have had a better understanding of the nature of mathematics, however.

Schmitz[69] examined the adequacy of mathematics and physical science library collections as well as their utilization by teachers in 54 Michigan high schools. Compiling a master list of 551 titles from standard bibliographic tools, she found that on the average only 8½ percent of these items were possessed by each media center. Moreover, 54 percent of the mathematics teachers indicated that they used the collection very little, while 25 percent didn't use it at all. Between 55 percent and 89 percent said they did not use any teaching method involving such materials.

Mack[70] surveyed the content of 13 educational periodicals for one year to determine the treatment given to the role of the school library. She found that the greatest attention was given to the media center in the language arts program. Less emphasis was given to it in science, social sciences, and special education and almost nothing was said regarding its potential in the other areas of the curriculum, including mathematics.

Most journal articles in the past have provided little or no mention of the media center's role in their treatment of mathematics instruction, but prefer to describe such factors as team teaching; some may possibly allude to the importance of having additional materials to supplement the lectures.[71] Not even in the description of seminars for gifted students, with their independent study emphasis, can we find any reference to use of the media center.[72] Others consider a number of relevant points and proceed to stress the wisdom in utilizing a variety of approaches,[73] recommend certain projects to be completed,[74] suggest grouping procedures for classes,[75] or encourage the stimulation of pupil interest,[76] all without mention of the possible utility of media centers and specialists. Even more discouraging than the infrequent recognition of the value of media is the lack of awareness or concern for the agency which organizes and disseminates them.[77]

The only critical analysis of the media center's role in mathematics was provided by two Englishmen in the early 1960s. Crosby and Percival relegate the difficulties in the utilization of library materials for teaching purposes to the operation of three important factors: (1) mathematics deals with symbols rather than words, (2) the media center has relatively few mathematics books at the secondary school level, and (3) one cannot gain an understanding of mathematics through biographies. "The background knowledge may add interest to the subject for many, but it does not directly improve mathematical skills or add to the systematic understanding of the subject, nor is it necessarily best acquired by the children in the library from books."[78]

This most interesting and provocative assessment of the media center's role is formulated with regard to a philosophical orientation which does not concede the necessity of peripheral activities related to the mastery of skills and operations; therefore, the media center can be only of minor importance. If it is true that acquisition of background knowledge and increased student interest in the subject are only incidental considerations to the teaching routine, the role of the media center in mathematics instruction is certainly a limited one. All writers do not concur with this analysis, however, as we shall see in the following pages.

THE MEDIA CENTER AS A MAJOR FACTOR IN MATHEMATICS INSTRUCTION

Recent writers have pointed to the necessity for the media specialist and mathematics teacher to cooperate in the selection of materials, preparation of assignments, and the teaching of reading and library skills peculiar to mathematics. They deplore the customary belief that in mathematics a textbook is sufficient, regarding it as a mistaken notion of the objectives of mathematics education which today is concerned with the discovery approach. This philosophy represents the media center as indispensable to the "discovery approach," and interprets the responsibility of the teacher to exceed that of teaching skills but rather to develop mathematical insight. Development of this insight requires a variety of materials.[79]

Meder promulgated this idea over a decade ago in his assertion that there really is no reason for mathematics teachers to use the library so long as the primary objective is regarded as skill in solving problems of predetermined type.[80] He then reveals the need for better goals and better teaching aimed at the development of understanding rather than the coverage of a body of material. He offers seven reasons why the mathematics teacher needs the library, which include provision of supplementary materials for individual needs and for bright students, development of interest and motivation, and coverage of topics that cannot be covered in class.

Taylor and Sparks[81] attributed the deficiencies of mathematics collections in school libraries to the relatively slight demand placed upon them, development of the collection being dependent upon the interest and activity of the teaching department. They suggest six broad areas of media center utilization in mathematics programs which closely resemble the seven reasons offered by Meder. They are: (1) creation of interest through recreational activities, (2) selection of mathematics projects, (3) use of media to supplement textbooks, (4) provision of materials for the gifted, (5) provision for the professional growth of teachers, and (6) provision of helpful procedures for the improvement of instruction.

Some writers have described their own programs which identified the media center as an aid in forming proper attitudes and increasing knowledge,[82] as well as a means of creating interest and encouraging independent study.[83] Others have stressed the utility of various materials in enhancing mathematical competency,[84] thus embracing the media center as an aid which is in total harmony with the emphasis in mathematics on skills of measurement, classification, observation, and experimentation.[85]

Through the years there have been several pleas for the mathematics teacher to take a more active role in teaching reading skills, if only to bring his pupils in contact with materials suitable to their level of comprehension.[86] This is in keeping with educational theory which would have every subject teacher become a teacher of reading; thus reading for enjoyment is important in mathematics for it would set the stage for more methodical reading related to skill mastery.[87] A good media center collection, therefore, necessarily would include various types of books such as general introductions, recreational mathematics, histories, applications, philosophy, and general references.[88]

Consideration of the role of the media center in mathematics is therefore not an uncommon topic for speculation and opinion among observers

46

and participants, although the area is certainly not as extensively treated as are some of the other important elements of this study. More important is the paucity of research efforts in this regard, and it is hoped that this study will help to bring a measure of understanding to a situation where it is needed.

Purposeful reading is seen to be beneficial by most writers, especially those actively supporting the media center role in mathematics instruction. The degree to which encouragement of this activity is related to mathematics instruction in terms of the teacher's role or his responsibility is dependent upon the writer's own philosophy of education. Most surprising, however, is the dearth of literature concerning the utilization of film material, the only reference being made several years ago to the usefulness of films and filmstrips by individuals or small groups when viewed outside of class in order to supplement classroom activity.[89]

In this review of related literature we have attempted to recreate for the reader the context out of which grew the subject matter of this book. The second part of the chapter explains in detail the nature and design of the study, indicating the influence of the literature in its determination. It should become apparent that the methodology and structural characteristics of the investigation result from an analysis of the problem in terms of its components and the treatment accorded these factors in the past.

II. Structuring the Study

Having established the problem, the next major task was to make our project viable by setting up a plan for collecting and analyzing the needed data. For researchers, the development of a useful methodology is a most trying and enervating activity. This is the foundation of any research effort, however; and the strength of the discovery is dependent upon the methods and techniques employed to gather the information and once gathered, the manner in which it is treated.

Let us begin by restating the hypothesis on which the research for this work was undertaken: *The greater the teacher utilization of media center resources in his teaching, the greater the use of the center by pupils, because in their recognition of the teacher as a subject-matter authority pupils will emulate his manner of acquiring knowledge and/or in their regard for the teacher as a desirable personality they will seek to please him.* Thus, the factors of personality and expertise of the teacher are proffered as the real reasons for a student undertaking to follow that teacher's suggestions with neither threat of punishment nor promise of reward.

Design and Procedures

Logical consequence four was chosen as the focal point of the study and is also restated here: *The heaviest circulation of materials is to pupils enrolled in courses taught by teachers who most often utilize such resources in their teaching.* In order to determine the influence of a subject-matter teacher on his pupils' use of the media center, we decided that the experimental design would be most efficacious. In this way, the amount or degree of teacher utilization of library materials could be measured precisely, and the number of bibliographic activities or reinforcements could be varied from week to week. Therefore, we were able to measure directly the effects of the teacher on pupils' use of those materials and thereby gain more insight into the real reasons for the differences in pupil reading patterns.

Not to belabor this point, we reiterate that the use of the experimental method distinguishes this study from those in the past which have been largely of descriptive nature. To be sure, these past studies have served a useful purpose in revealing variables and describing the situation as it exists. The time has come, however, when an experimental approach can be implemented and thus the variable of teacher utilization is identified as the change agent upon which pupil use of nonrequired materials is dependent.

We employed the familiar "before-after" technique involving both experimental and control groups. The "before" measurement is rendered by a pretest of six weeks in which use of the library by all pupils is recorded, while the "after" measurement is the record of library use obtained during the test period of eight weeks. Also included is a subsequent period of six weeks duration in which the carryover effects are observed. Whether or not the students would continue to use materials once the teacher ceased to encourage them was an important question with which to contend. The ramifications have been discussed previously in terms of the development of lifelong users of the library.

The framework for this study and the procedures employed found their basis in numerous writings of the past, many of which have been described in preceding pages. In promulgating the theory that the teacher is responsible for motivating pupils to read beyond the text assignment and that library use is dependent upon the aims and objectives of the curriculum, Hartz has provided directly the manner for testing our hypothesis: "The reference to a number of good books in the field, as well as references to specific chapters and pages, is more valuable than the vague comment: The library has a few good books on the subject."[90]

During the test period the experimental group received attention from the teacher in its course-related bibliographic pursuits. He detailed in precise fashion the pages or sections of mathematics items relevant to work in class and encouraged their use. During this eight-week period four book titles were presented weekly (two concept development titles, one a recreational title, and one a historical or background title). One film or filmstrip title and one periodical article also were included to determine if any differences exist in students' preferences, for a total of six items per week.

PRELIMINARY DECISIONS

The design of the study reveals itself in a series of preliminary decisions which were necessary before data collecting could begin. These decisions which represented much deliberation and thought were demonstrated in the selection of the academic discipline, the school, the teacher, and the titles for inclusion in the bibliography.

Choice of academic subject. The first decision involved the choice of subject. As noted in the first chapter, we felt that the importance of the study would be manifest if results were positive in certain skill areas categorized previously as minor library users by the National Education Association project in 1958. A more complete understanding of the media center's role in these areas is crucial for the direction of future efforts. According to Klohn, "there is no area of study for which it is impossible to obtain library materials. The supply depends upon demands made by the teacher; frequent demand increases supply."[91]

There is some evidence that knowledgeable people are of this mind. An example is the questionnaire study conducted by Walker of the faculties at two high schools which were part of the original Knapp project. It was found that 66 percent of the teachers and 66 percent of the librarians disagreed with the statement that the library and its resources are more essential to English and social studies than to other areas.[92] Burbank feels that all teachers should constantly refer to books. "If books are discussed in classes, all classes, not just the obviously book-oriented social studies and English classes, how can students resist for long investigating at least a few of those mentioned?"[93] In our case we would wish to expand that question to include other types of media as well as books.

Mathematics became a logical choice. We have already shown the neglect of this discipline with regard to school library or media center objectives, focus, and activity. Rossoff doesn't even mention mathematics in his library manual, not even under the subheading, "Other Subject Areas."[94] For their part, mathematics educators do not generally regard the library as an important resource in the implementation of the curriculum. This situation mandates careful scrutiny.

Choice of school. The second major decision turned on the homogeneity of the student body as an important criterion used in selection of the school. Since a school situation would preclude the possibility of random selection of sample members we naturally felt that as close a match as possible should exist between the experimental and control groups within the school. To hold constant the contaminating effects of different home backgrounds, abilities, and interests of the students we decided that a laboratory school of a university would best serve, although a high school of medium or small size located in a homogeneous suburban community would suffice.

University High School, the laboratory school of the University of Illinois and the first choice of the author, approved of the proposal for study; and it was here that the experiment was conducted. The choice was a fortunate one for a number of reasons, the first of which was the pronounced homogeneity of the pupils illustrated in following pages. A second reason lies in the philosophical orientation of the school which encourages observation and experimentation. Not only were cooperation and certain staff services provided graciously, but the pupils were accustomed to being observed by a variety of people. Therefore, the author was confident that they were not sensitized by his presence.

There was another equally important consideration which relates also to the choice of mathematics as the subject. University High School enjoys a unique advantage in its connection with the University of Illinois Curriculum on School Mathematics. Nationally known for its work in shaping and reshaping the school mathematics curriculum, UICSM employs teachers of outstanding ability, innovativeness, and creativity, engaged in producing texts, workbooks, and guides. These teachers receive rank in the Department of Secondary and Continuing Education at the University, as do all teachers at the High School. As one might expect, there is an extensive collection of mathematics materials from which we were able to compile the necessary bibliographies.

Choice of teacher and pupils. According to Blakeway, "There are three ways to supplement basal texts: (1) with other books, (2) with an effective teacher, and (3) with a subtle combination of both these methods."[95] The third decision involved the choice of teacher and through making this choice a concomitant selection of the sample. One teacher was to be chosen for an in-depth analysis of his effects on the voluntary reading activity of pupils in two of his classes. The use of one teacher rather than two would naturally preclude the necessity of matching teachers on pertinent characteristics. In a meeting with the head of the mathematics de-

50

partment at the school, we presented him with a list of requirements of the attributes of the teacher to be studied (Appendix A).

We have already conceptualized the importance of expertise and personality in the composition of the effective teacher, and therein lay the basis of our request. The department chairman identified one individual who he felt fulfilled all stated requirements to the letter and when approached by the author, Mr. T readily agreed to the proposed research.

In selecting the teacher, the subjects or members of the sample were automatically chosen. These were the pupils in two of his classes at the subfreshman (or junior high school) level, each group consisting of 17 pupils. Included among their number were one high school freshman in the experimental group and two freshmen in the control group. These individuals were new entrants to the school and were required to take the first year course in mathematics which differs from the curriculum of more conventional institutions. The students of each class were assigned by the administration in more or less random manner, described by the school principal as the "pin-prick technique."

We were presented with a unique opportunity for comparative purposes with the consideration of a third subfreshman group of 16 pupils taught by Miss M. The students in this group had been purposely selected by the administration because of their relatively lower mathematics achievement grades. Due to the special circumstances involved in the selection and composition of this class, it was not used as another control group per se. Data were kept, however, for comparison with the other two groups and thereby the entire subfreshman population of University High School was included in the study.

Choice of bibliography. The final preliminary decision involved the selection of a suitable bibliography for presentation by the teacher. We decided that four book titles falling under three categories would be presented each week: two titles would be related to conceptual development or mastery of techniques, one title would represent recreational literature, and one title would be of historical or background type. In addition, there would be included each week one film or filmstrip title and one periodical article in order to determine if there were preferences for nonbook material on the part of the pupils. The weekly bibliography would thus number six annotated pertinent items.

Previously mentioned were the benefits accruing to the effort from the unique relationship between University High School and the University of Illinois Curriculum on School Mathematics in terms of the availability of mathematics materials. Next door to the high school, UICSM maintains a separate library facility which is accessible to pupils and faculty. It is a superb collection of mathematics materials and related items at all levels of understanding and surpasses by far the average high school collection in quantity and quality. We borrowed most of the titles appearing on the weekly bibliographies from UICSM and placed them on reserve in the media center of University High. Circulation records were checked at UICSM in the same manner as were those at the high school, although no loans were recorded there during the study.

We conducted a thorough search of materials relating to elementary algebra and geometry pertinent to the curriculum. The two most important tools were the recent publications of the National Council of Teachers of Mathematics, *The High School Mathematics Library* by Schaaf and *Mathematics Library: Elementary and Junior High School* by Hardgrove and Miller. The other sources were the Wilson publications, *Junior High School Library Catalog*, with supplements, and *Senior High School Library Catalog*, with supplements, and the American Library Association's *Basic Book Collection for Junior High Schools.*

We decided to make use of the knowledge of library materials possessed by 90 teachers of junior high school level mathematics who were attending the UICSM Summer Institute. A questionnaire (*see* Appendix B) was given to each participant in which he was asked to indicate any titles which he held in high regard. Although the response was slight (only 15 questionnaires were returned), about 30 books were recommended. All of these were considered but most were eliminated later when the topics for coverage during the test period were finally determined. Even so, six of the 32 book titles used in the study were first suggested here. Although no periodical articles were recommended, the names of three relevant journals were provided. An added bonus of this instrument lay in the fact that in its second part we made our initial attempt to examine the phenomenon of causality. This aspect will be covered more fully later in this chapter.

Most trying was the constant focus on providing a relevant and valuable bibliography. This occupied the greater part of the author's time during the conduct of the experiment. Final selections were made by the author with the approval of Mr. T on a week-to-week basis just prior to their presentation in class. The eight weekly bibliographies used appear in Appendix C.

The majority of the periodical articles were taken from various issues of *Arithmetic Teacher*. The two concept film loops were borrowed from the UICSM collection and recommended by Mr. T, as were the three filmstrips from Eyegate, edited by Jo Phillips of the UICSM staff. The three filmstrips from SVE were purchased by the author after preview and approval by Mr. T. The use of nonbook material was analyzed primarily on the basis of form rather than content and compared in general fashion to the totality of book use, although some interesting and important facts are brought to light in chapter 4 regarding the content of this material.

52

THE SIX-WEEK PRETEST

The school term began in September and the first six weeks were used as a pretest serving several purposes. Most important was the determination of any differences which existed between the students in Mr. T's two classes in their use of the library. Since a coin toss had established the second period class (8:54–9:44) as the experimental group and the fifth period class (11:36–12:26) as the control, we felt it necessary to ascertain to what extent they made use of the library without any encouragement from Mr. T. Therefore, records were kept of all subfreshman library loans including those of Miss M's class. Of course, the circulation of mathematics titles is of primary importance, but we did not limit our study to those alone.

Another important purpose served by the pretest was suggested by the head of the mathematics department. This was in part to enable the pupils, all of whom were new to the school, to acclimate themselves to the new environment, and in part to permit Mr. T to establish the type of rapport with the students which we considered necessary to success.

The third purpose served by the six-week period lay in the establishment of the techniques of the study. Since daily observation of both Mr. T's classes had been planned for the test period, this was an ideal opportunity for the author to make his presence as an observer known to the pupils. Both classes were observed each Thursday of the pretest for the full six weeks, thereby lessening any effect that such observations would have during the test period.

It was thought that this type of scheduled appearance would better serve to identify the author as a regular visitor than would sporadic visitation. Introduced as an "observer from the University who would be around for a while in order to witness different methods of teaching junior high school youngsters," he was thus disengaged from any primary association with the mathematics department. This factor was helpful later in eliciting truthful responses from the pupils on the interview and rating scale.

At the outset, the control group appeared to be more aggressive, energetic, and eager, although it was obvious that both groups were bright and knowledgeable. In the ensuing weeks, the experimental group showed great gains in animated behavior, and by the end of the fifth week both classes seemed to conduct themselves in much the same manner. More important, both groups had come to accept the author as a regular visitor and to disregard his presence.

By the end of the pretest, it was apparent that Mr. T was a fine teacher who brought out the best efforts of his pupils and had created the desired type of classroom atmosphere. The study of congruence was to begin on schedule, and the first weekly bibliography was employed during the

53

seventh week of school (the first week of our test period). It was at this time that both classes were told by Mr. T that in the next few weeks helpful mathematics materials would be placed on reserve in the media center.

Also important was the perfection of data collection routines during this time. A student library aide, a girl of junior standing, was recommended by the librarian as being especially reliable and efficient. It was her task to go through the daily circulation at the close of day, remove the book cards of subfreshman borrowers, and record these entries by means of photocopying (about four or five cards to the page). These photocopied pages were then placed in a folder at the circulation desk and recorded later by the investigator. A complete record was thus provided which included all instances of use, whether regular or reserve, home or room charge. This pattern for collection of data worked quite well from the beginning.

The Eight-Week Test Period

The pattern for observation and collection of data had been established during the pretest and was successfully continued through the test period of the experiment. Neither experimental nor control group pupils seemed to notice that the author now was attending classes on a daily rather than the earlier weekly basis. As was true of the school in general, visitors frequently had attended these classes for varying lengths of time during the preceding weeks, and the author appeared to be a visitor with no special purpose other than an interest in observing the teaching methods employed in subfreshman courses.

Teacher utilization. In observing the classes daily, it was possible to note the type of encouragement or manner of influence provided to the experimental group by Mr. T. Records were kept of the amount of time (number of minutes) that such encouragement or reinforcement was given, and the number of reinforcements was deliberately changed from week to week. Mr. T expressed a preference for an introductory session to be held each Monday in which the use of all six titles was to be encouraged, and pupils were to receive the bibliography handout for the week. He would then provide reinforcement in accordance with the needs of the study. Of course nothing was to be said to the control group, nor were the bibliographies to be given to its membership.

This proved to be a desirable procedure for inclusion of the independent variable, combining the preferences of the teacher with the needs of the investigator. Moreover, it provided for the pupils the type of regularity which is expected of school practices, assuring the pupils that the bibliographic effort was the concern of the teacher and not of an outside party.

Therefore, the bibliographies were distributed by Mr. T as part of his normal teaching routine.

It was most important at this time to convey properly the idea of voluntary or nonrequired reading as opposed to assignments. This was first mentioned in the brief remarks made to both classes at the close of the pretest, and reiterated several times throughout the test period to the experimental group. All pupils in the group were encouraged to use the materials on their bibliographies since it was in their best interest to do so. Mr. T made it quite clear that while he hoped that these materials would be used, he would not require it. Pupils' grades would not be affected in any way by their use or nonuse, nor would any tests be given on this material.

All items on the bibliography had been approved in advance by Mr. T during planning sessions held prior to the test period. In these sessions, we had reached agreement on the study procedures and were assured of a listing of materials which were readable and informative, as well as relevant to the course of study.

Each Monday, prior to presentation, we reviewed the items for the week and the points of emphasis to be made. This served to refresh Mr. T's memory with respect to the materials, and enabled him to question any aspect and to suggest further pursuits. Mr. T brought the materials to class, showed them to the pupils and encouraged them to make use of the items. The titles were than placed in the school library on reserve, with circulation privileges on an overnight basis after 3 P.M.

It soon became apparent that the type of influence exerted by Mr. T differed inasmuch as three different levels of personal involvement on his part could be identified. Therefore, three different ploys (generally informative, hopeful, and disappointed) were categorized and did represent an ascending order of teacher involvement. (That is, the teacher was most involved when he acted disappointed in their failure to read and least involved when he simply informed the students of the materials.) The reinforcements were duly recorded as were the total number of minutes spent on the subject of books. It should be stated here that, in our reference to greater degree of utilization by the teacher, we were not overly concerned with the number of reinforcements per week, and even less so with the number of minutes per activity. More pertinent in demonstrating the effects of a stimulus such as an effective teacher was the consistent mention and encouragement offered over a long period of time (in this case, eight weeks). The number of reinforcements was purposely varied for comparisons on the immediate effects and served to add another dimension to the effort.

Collection of data. As mentioned previously, the routines for data collection had been introduced in the pretest. The student assistant checked the daily circulation, removed all cards representing subfreshman charges, and recorded the entries by photocopying them. All types of materials loaned by the library were checked and recorded, producing a complete record of library use for the entire subfreshman class. When combined with the records of the pretest, we were able to determine the kinds of changes which occurred within and between the three groups with respect to library use for the first fourteen weeks of the school year.

We readily concede that circulation records do not necessarily represent use of the materials; for this reason provision was made for a check on such use in the construction of the interview schedule. With such a check present, it must be agreed that no better indicator of pupil use of library materials exists than that which represents the contract between user and library. Even if *all* items charged out were not used faithfully by the borrower, library circulation was still an effect of teacher utilization. If it could be shown that *any* items were read, the goal or purpose of the study would then have been achieved.

The Six-Week Post-Test

The post-test began one week prior to Christmas vacation and continued for five weeks into the new year. It was introduced into the experiment for two equally important reasons. First, it would serve to show whether a change would take place within the control group with respect to their use of mathematics materials, once having been apprised by a neutral party of the location and availability of these items, the neutral party being the author who so informed each pupil in interviews that took place during the Christmas vacation. If it could be shown that this bibliographic awareness or guidance was not enough to motivate these pupils to use the materials, the case for teacher influence as the real stimulus would necessarily be strengthened.

Even more important, possibly, was the degree to which mathematics materials would be used by members of the experimental group once the teacher ceased to encourage such activity. Would there be any carryover or residual effects of teacher influence or would conditions be much the same as they were prior to the test period?

At the time of the interview, the author informed pupils of the control group of the location, availability, and usefulness of the mathematics books which were still on reserve in the library. In an appeal to their competitive nature, they were also told that Mr. T's other class had been using these materials extensively over the past two months. The Christmas recess, happily, served as a natural break between the test period and the greater part of the post-test, an easy transition thus being achieved between the period of intense involvement and saturation with materials to complete withdrawal on the part of the teacher with the experimental group. Also, the sensitizing influence of the interviews was allowed to lessen in the time prior to the beginning of school, since the interviews were completed by December 23.

During the post-test, Mr. T refrained from mentioning books to either group. The author no longer sat in attendance of the class sessions and removed himself as much as possible from the school premises. Weekly sessions with Mr. T were held in which the conduct of the class was discussed and the author gained assurance that no mention was being made of the materials. During the final week of the post-test Mr. T reported an inadvertent mention of a book title to the experimental group. The fact that this was made known to the author served to reassure him of the veracity of his assumption that Mr. T had not referred to books at any other time during this period.

Data regarding library use were collected in the usual manner and thereby served to provide a complete record of library use for the entire subfreshman class over a period of twenty weeks. It was therefore possible to compare, analyze, and interpret on the basis of a fairly extensive record.

The School and the Pupils

The criteria employed in selecting the school have already been explained and concern primarily the homogeneity of the student body. In the choice of University High School, we felt reasonably assured that certain contaminating effects were held as constant as possible in the teaching situation. That is to say, pupils in both the control and experimental groups resembled each other closely in terms of their personal characteristics. This section provides a brief description of the school and a comparison of the pupils.

University High School and the Subfreshman Program

Since 1921, University High School has been operating as the laboratory school of the College of Education at the University of Illinois. One of its major functions is to experiment with the content, methods, and materials of secondary education. For this reason it attracts exceptional teachers as well as exceptional pupils. These teachers receive faculty rank in the College of Education and are encouraged to be creative and innovative in teaching their subjects and to explore these subjects in greater depth and with greater sophistication than would be possible in the usual secondary school.

Classes are small, the student population remaining constant at 250. This is important for the type of close pupil-teacher relationship which is considered necessary to such a program. The pupils are selected carefully on the basis of above-average academic ability as demonstrated by their performance on a battery of tests administered prior to gaining admission. Few students are admitted who are not basically capable of meeting the demands of a rigorous academic program. The general structure is of a five-year program beginning with the subfreshman year which combines both seventh- and eighth-grade learnings.

The subfreshman class, with which this study is concerned, is limited to not more than 50 members. They must have completed sixth grade with favorable aptitude and achievement records, secured parental approval for entering University High School, and be of normal emotional development. These pupils characteristically rank within the top ten percent of their elementary school classes in scholastic ability and intelligence. If a student has completed seventh grade, he may not enter the subfreshman class, and very few are accepted beyond this level.

In addition to mathematics, subjects required of subfreshmen include English and social studies on a daily basis throughout the academic year, while science and music are half-year offerings usually taken alternately. Latin may be chosen as an extra major while art, home economics, and industrial arts complete the list of courses which may be chosen to establish the pupil's complete program. There is no tuition charge, although there is a nominal activity fee as well as additional charges for textbooks, laboratory fees, and supplies.

The subfreshman program, then, serves as an example of a successful accelerated plan, one which had its beginning in 1932. It represents for the pupils an opportunity to participate in an educational endeavor unique in its stability, academic excellence, and continuity and reflecting the best thinking in terms of sequential planning and development. The selectivity of the admission policy and the orientation to innovation and experimentation afforded a unique opportunity for the purposes of this study.

THE SAMPLE

In choosing University High School for the experiment, it was clear that the sample would be a biased one in terms of pupils' abilities due to the selective process for admission to the school. As was pointed out in the first chapter, however, this bias was not an unfortunate element in the development of the study. Although we did not consider it necessary that the sample should represent extraordinary abilities or high acumen, this aspect is advantageous in several ways.

First, we are assured of the best possible effects of the independent variable in working with what may be considered to be the upper register of the total population of youngsters of this age and grade level. If teacher utilization of library materials is ever a truly effective stimulant to pupils in their use of those materials, evidence should be forthcoming with the employment of this sample. The fact that positive results could be expected more readily with this group than with a class of more normal composition then provides an effective determinant for further study.

If the present effort were to show positive results, the natural question would then be posed as to its application for groups in more normal circumstances. Replication should then ensue in the logical quest for scientific truth. On the other hand, negative results with above-average pupils would effectively label teacher utilization as an unimportant device, one requiring little further study. This type of definitive conclusion could not be realized in a test of normally constituted groups which showed negative results, since the question would then be asked of the effects on better endowed individuals.

Of the total subfreshman class of 50 pupils, 34 were studied in depth due to their placement in either the control or experimental group. Each group contained 17 members, the experimental group meeting with Mr. T earlier in the morning than did the control group. The remaining 16 pupils had been selected by the administration for Miss M's class because they all had lower mathematics achievement scores. As a result, they are not part of the control group. Their use of the library was recorded in order to make comparisons with both the experimental and control groups.

As we have stated, the major concern was the relative homogeneity of the control and experimental groups. Both groups were to be of similar abilities and character. Other variables were to be held as constant as was possible in a school situation. Six personal factors were identified and compared: sex, age, IQ, mathematics achievement, reading achievement, and father's education. One school condition, the number of free periods, was also identified. The pupils are compared on these characteristics, and insight is provided into the composition of the two groups and their remarkable similarity. It was not considered necessary to use any techniques other than a comparison of means and ranges on the characteristics. Tables 1 and 2 provide the necessary information.

Sex. The two groups consisted of 20 girls and 14 boys. There was a slightly disproportionate composition in each group. The experimental group had 11 girls and 6 boys, while the control group was composed of 9 girls and 8 boys. There was no way to judge the effects of this slight difference on the results of the experiment. In the code used for table 1 and succeeding tables, B represents boys and G, girls.

TABLE 1. SEVEN CHARACTERISTICS OF THE EXPERIMENTAL GROUP MEMBERS, WITH GROUP MEANS AND RANGES

SEX AND CODE NUMBER BOYS/GIRLS	AGE IN MONTHS	VERBAL IQ	MATH ACHIEVEMENT GRADE LEVEL	READING ACHIEVEMENT PERCENTILE	FATHER'S EDUCATION*	NO. OF FREE PERIODS PER DAY
B1	144	137	10.0+	76	4	0
G3	150	126	9.3	85	4	0
B8	144	150	10.0+	99	4	0
G11	142	133	9.3	95	4	0
G14	146	137	10.0+	89	4	0
G15	144	144	10.0+	95	1	0
B14	145	144	8.3	92	2	0
G16	149	137	9.3	98	4	0
G17	150	131	8.7	81	3	0
B16	142	123	8.0	63	1	1
G19	141	145	10.0+	97	4	0
G20	145	139	8.8	92	3	0
B23	165	150	—	99	4	2
G22	153	129	10.0+	85	4	0
B21	152	146	10.0+	85	4	1
G23	151	130	8.5	70	3	0
G24	143	148	8.8	99	4	0
Mean	147.47	138.18	9.31	88.24	3.35	.24
Range	24	27	2.0	29	3	2

*Scale: 1 = No degree; 2 = Bachelor's; 3 = Master's; 4 = Doctorate

Age. The mean age for members of both groups was 148.21 months. Although there was a difference between the groups in age range, the distinctions were slight between them when averaged out. These differences were unlikely to produce any changes with regard to library use by the groups, and for all practical purposes the groups were homogeneous on this aspect. The slight advantage was seen to reside in the control group.

Verbal IQ. Prior to admission to school, the pupils were tested on the Lorge-Thorndike Intelligence Test yielding a score for verbal intelligence and a score for nonverbal intelligence. The former was used for purposes of comparison. Again, the difference between the groups was slight and quite unlikely to produce any distinctions in library use, the slender advantage again belonging to the control group.

Mathematics achievement. The arithmetic section of the Metropolitan Achievement Test was also administered to the pupils prior to their admission to school. This produced a score for each pupil representing his mathematics ability in terms of grade level, and did not register an ability beyond tenth grade. Therefore, the score of 10.0+ is the highest possible score, attained by eight members of the control group and seven members of the experimental group. The three individuals of freshman rank were not tested on this variable; therefore the means were based on 15 scores in the control group and 16 scores in the experimental group. Again, there was little difference between the two groups and the very slight distinction was again in favor of the control group.

Reading achievement. The Cooperative English Examination was administered to all pupils as part of the battery of tests. This yielded a range or band of percentile rankings. Since this test was standardized on ninth-graders, it is the policy of the school to represent the highest percentile rank in the band as the individual's score. It is with respect to this trait that the most obvious distinction exists between the groups. The mean for the control group was 92.65 as compared to 88.24 for the experimental group. This represents a difference of 4.41 percentiles or just under 5 percent of the mean total for both groups, a somewhat greater gap than was present in the comparison of other traits. Whatever the difference, the impact on the study is negligible since the advantage again is in favor of the control group.

Father's education. The final characteristic was that of the educational level of the head of the household to which the pupils belong. It has been used in past studies in education to explain differences in motivations for study as demonstrated by various pupils. It is of dubious value to this study since one of the requirements for admission to University High School is parental support of the program. In visiting all the pupils in their homes, we did not feel that any real difference existed in terms of family motiva-

TABLE 2. COMPARISON OF GROUP CHARACTERISTICS OF PUPILS

| | SEX | | MEAN AGE | MEAN |
	BOYS	GIRLS	IN MONTHS	IQ
Experimental	6	11	147.47	138.18
Control	8	9	148.94	138.71
Both Groups	14	20	148.21	138.44

tion. All pupils were expected to perform to the best of their ability, and in all households it was considered an important task. Data on this aspect were recorded chiefly to provide as much background information as possible on pupils in the sample.

Using an arbitrary scale of four points for a doctorate, three points for a master's degree, two points for a bachelor's, and one point for no college degree, the father's education was evaluated in all but three cases. In these three cases, all in the control group, the mother's occupation was used, since she was the head of the family. No distinction was accorded to type of doctorate; thus Ph.D., M.D., and J.D. all received the same weight.

It is interesting that in this, the characteristic felt to be of least importance, we see the only advantage held by the experimental group. It was not, however, expected to provide any basis for distinction in use of the library by pupils.

Homogeneity. The tables and description of the pupil's characteristics are presented in order to provide insight into the degree of success in finding relatively homogenous groups in an existing school situation. Clearly, there is very little to distinguish one group from another, the difference in every case being slight and inconsequential. These differences, moreover, in every case but one are in favor of the control group, the one exception being in the area of the father's education, not considered to be as important as the other characteristics. In summation, there is no reason to think that were the situation to have been reversed, the control group members having been chosen to receive the independent variable, that their performance would not have been just as positive.

Free time as a variable. One more characteristic judged to be of major importance in a comparison of the two groups was the inclusion of study periods in their daily schedule. This factor deserves special consideration for two reasons; first, it is an environmental condition rather than a personal quality and second, it concerns directly the important concept of accessibility. Since accessibility has long been recognized as one of the chief determinants of media center use, it would naturally be important to

MEAN MATH GRADE LEVEL	MEAN READING PERCENTILE	MEAN FATHER'S EDUCATION	MEAN NO. DAILY FREE PERIODS
9.31	88.24	3.35	.24
9.39	92.65	2.88	.75
9.35	90.44	3.12	.49

discover which pupils have greater access to the center's resources by virtue of having free periods during the school day. It is both interesting and important to note the great difference in favor of the control group in this regard.

Only three pupils in the experimental group had any free periods at all between 8 A.M. and 3:30 P.M., the regular school day, while free periods were included in the schedule of 11 members of the control group. The mean for the control group was 0.75 daily, while the mean for the experimental group was 0.24, fully 0.51 less than the control or more than 100 percent of the total mean. Obviously, the groups were quite dissimilar in this respect, and just as obvious is the fact that should the performance of the experimental group be positive in nature, it would represent the overcoming of a barrier. That is, if the experimental group read more materials than did the control, it would be in spite of the fact that these materials were relatively inaccessible to the members of that group. Since the only opportunity to use the library for individuals without free periods was at lunch time or after school until 4 P.M. when the library closed, it reflects a major effort on their part. In brief, it points to a rather strong effect of teacher motivation.

Professional Responsibility—Teacher and Media Specialist

THE SEARCH FOR CAUSALITY

We have already alluded to the difficulty in finding reasons for the acceptance of teacher's suggestions. This complexity is demonstrated in our choice of two possible causes of which either one or both may apply to the particular case and when taken together represent teacher influence.

This does not mean we are saying that teacher influence alone, however broadly interpreted, can possibly encompass all reasons for positive reactions on the part of pupils to the activities of their teacher. Quite apart from a consideration of the teacher's characteristics is the necessary examination of the traits of the pupils, which in the past have received primary attention in studies of teaching effects. This, of course, helps to explain our concern for the relative homogeneity of the control and experimental groups in this study.

Other possible causes. To be sure, there are at least three factors which may affect the use of nonrequired materials by pupils other than the teacher's influence, the first being the guidance element. Here, guidance is demonstrated in the compilation and preparation of well-structured and topical bibliographies pinpointing the relevant aspects of the materials in such a way as to be economical of students' time. The question, then, is whether or not students would use materials if such awareness were provided by a person deemed not to be influential.

A second factor is the student's satisfaction with previously used materials which again might be considered apart from the person who suggests their use. If the youngster feels that he has derived some benefit from the use of such materials in the past, there would normally be a greater propensity to use them.

The third factor is the interest that the student has for the subject. If genuinely interested in the content of the course, chances for extracurricular pursuits such as outside reading are definitely enhanced, no matter who has charge of the class. Immediately, one can see that the first factor of guidance is similar to teacher influence in its being a teacher consideration while satisfaction with materials and subject interest are pupil traits and thereby more closely related to each other.

In this study we favored the inclusion of guidance under the category of teacher influence. Who can deny that preparation of lessons which involve consultation of outside resources is part of a teacher's responsibility? There is a similar responsibility to encourage constructive pupil effort outside the classroom. In doing this, there is a need to make students aware of useful learning devices of all types. The awareness of the pupil is achieved through guidance on the part of the teacher. The influence that a teacher wields in his relationship with pupils is necessarily enhanced by the information he provides them with respect to the existence of such aids. Guidance thus forms a rung on the ladder of influence and, for our purposes, need not be separated.

Other things being equal, the presence of an influential teacher who promotes the use of outside materials in one class and not in the other becomes the crucial factor in the comparison of the use of those materials by the two classes. Guidance is part of the equipment in the teacher's effectiveness. We did, however, institute a partial control on the guidance factor in this study when, at the close of the pretest, pupils in both groups were made aware of the fact that books would be placed on reserve by the teacher in the next few weeks.

A strong reinforcement also was rendered at the beginning of the post-test when members of the control group were told by the author while interviewing them that mathematics books had been on reserve for several weeks and had been used extensively by Mr. T's other class. Thus, general awareness of the location and availability of the math books were provided, although it is true that the written bibliographies giving specific detail were not.

With respect to the second factor, the pupils' satisfaction with materials, the interview provided insight into the feelings of students regarding the usefulness of the items they had read. Of course, this factor could not account for the first use but must necessarily be considered in their repeated use or subsequent neglect of the materials. The third factor, subject interest, although a pupil trait rather than a teacher characteristic, has been found by Cogan to be related also to the student's feeling for the teacher.[96]

According to Bernstein, "We have all experienced a teacher whom we have greatly admired and with whom we either worked closely or for whom we did a great deal of extra work. By the opposite side of the coin many students have learned to dislike a subject simply on the basis of a personal relationship with an individual teacher."[97] Thus the relationship to a teacher and enjoyment of a subject are not entirely distinct factors and teacher influence would appear to bear heavily on subject interest. The rating scale employed here at the time of the interview provides a measure of the student's interest in mathematics. We would not expect it to differ radically from the admiration accorded the teacher.

Place of the media specialist. In developing the rationale and design of the study with its focus on the teacher's role, the place of the media specialist emerges with some clarity. It is our contention that the media specialist represents to the student the neutral level of involvement when linked to the use of curriculum-related materials. We do not deprecate this condition, but simply regard it as an aspect of the real world. The task, then, is to define the professional responsibility in view of its ramifications.

This does not appear to be difficult to do when the predominant role of the teacher is considered in motivating students to use the media center. If it is the teacher who establishes a favorable climate for library appreciation, we are then moved to ask, "Who motivates and influences the teacher?" The place of the media specialist, although secondary in terms of student interface, is of first importance as it relates to the teacher. In effect the media specialist influences the influencer and stimulates the stimulus.

INSTRUMENTS USED

Let us now look at the different data collection devices and the manner in which they were employed. In our effort to explain adequately the important phenomenon of teacher-pupil-media specialist interaction, it is important that our instruments provide us with meaningful information.

Questionnaire. Although in the questionnaire to the UICSM Summer Institute registrants (Appendix B) we were primarily interested in suggestions of titles for the bibliography, we also wanted some idea of what teachers thought were the reasons that students followed their suggestions. Therefore, the second question was framed to get their opinions regarding the pupils' use of nonrequired mathematics materials. Although this was an exploratory operation and rather crudely conducted, we did feel that any help in this regard would be welcome.

On the basis of this questionnaire, we were able to state earlier in this chapter that pupil characteristics generally receive more attention than do teacher characteristics in an analysis of teacher-pupil relationships. Thirty-six responses were identified from 15 teachers, only three of which could be said to represent teacher influence. Another four categories were identified, all of which reflected pupil traits: (1) the desire for enrichment or background knowledge, (2) desire for skill mastery, (3) desire for enjoyment, and (4) subject interest.

Most enlightening was the discovery that teachers place such little emphasis on their own role in getting pupils to use supplementary materials and would rather assess the phenomenon in terms of the personal qualities and intrinsic motivations of the pupils.

Rating scale. This instrument (Appendix D) was given to the students in both classes on an individual basis in the privacy of their own homes at the time of the interviews, and is concerned wholly with the nature of causality in the study. In the first question the pupils are asked to rate all their teachers on the two elements considered by the author to be the most important characteristics of an influential or effective teacher: (a) subject matter expertise with the ability to transmit knowledge to the pupils, and (b) desirable personality.

The responses to this question and the positioning of Mr. T in comparison to other teachers made it possible to build a case supporting our claims. If the results of the experiment were positive and it is suspected that the reasons lie in the personal qualities of the teacher, then it would be expected that Mr. T would rank relatively high in the estimation of his pupils.

The second question attempts to assess the pupil characteristic of subject interest which we have discussed as another possible reason for pupils' voluntary efforts. If the groups were shown to be similar in their attitudes toward mathematics, such attitudes by themselves then could not be said to account for differences in the use of mathematics materials between groups.

Since the rating scale required the representation of opinions which could be damaging to the respondent, the pupils were assured that the information provided would be of confidential nature and would not be divulged to others. It was here that our status was most helpful as a party interested in the general curriculum rather than mathematics specifically. Certainly, the pupils would not have been so candid in estimating the effectiveness of their teachers if the opposite were true. The rating scale was given to the pupil at the beginning of our interview before any specific mention of mathematics was made. Interview and rating scale together took an average of 30 to 40 minutes.

Pupil interviews. We scheduled the interviews in the homes of the pupils during the Christmas vacation through an official letter bearing the signature of the school principal (Appendix G). Obviously the advantages of home scheduling other than those already cited were that, in an unhurried and secure environment, the pupils would be more apt to provide truthful responses. Also, there would be much less intercourse between pupils regarding the nature of the interviews. Since the author was thought to be interested in the entire subfreshman program, he explained his preoccupation with the mathematics class in the interview as stemming from the fact that it was in this class that the particular pupil had been observed. The pupils apparently accepted this explanation without reservation.

The interviews with the members of the experimental group (Appendix E) were primarily concerned with their reasons for using the materials, the third question being especially important. The fourth and seventh questions were to ascertain the degree of satisfaction experienced by the pupils in their use of these library materials and therefore relate to another possible factor in student motivation.

The first two questions examine the pupils' attitudes toward bibliographic activity of the mathematics teacher; the last three questions consider the pupils' attitudes on the use of books and film material in mathematics and on the use of these materials in other subjects. The sixth question is important in that it serves as a check on the actual use of materials by pupils to whom they were charged. If it can be shown that at least one title was actually read, the library circulation pattern could be more readily accepted as a valid indicator of pupil use.

One important purpose in conducting the interviews with the control group was to make them aware of the availability of mathematics materials on reserve in the library. This, in effect, became a slight measure of guidance provided them by a neutral party, this researcher, and has already been described in preceding pages. Also, we were interested in determining how closely the opinions of this group coincided with those of the experimental group with respect to the use of supplementary materials. Possibly the most direct approach was found in question 5 which asked why it was that the students did not think to use library materials in mathematics more often. The results of these interviews and their implications are examined more fully in chapter 4.

Treatment of the Data

We assumed that four different categories of data interpretation were needed to demonstrate the results. These categories employed three different tests of significance. Due to the small size of the sample and its unique character, it became a matter of great importance to determine suitable techniques for statistical analysis. The t-test, a parametric technique possible with small samples, is useful only in cases for which one can assume a normally distributed population. This, according to Blalock, is difficult to do, since "it is when samples are small that we are ordinarily most in doubt about the exact nature of the population."[98] He refers to nonparametric tests, which do not involve the assumption of normality and could conceivably replace the t-test altogether in the future.

The use of nonparametric tests is encouraged by Barnes in his guide to the conduct of experiments in education when he points out that these techniques "seem reasonably well fitted to research projects undertaken in individual school systems, individual schools, and individual classrooms."[99]

> Nonparametric or distribution-free techniques require fewer qualifications and assumptions regarding the shape of the population. In testing hypotheses about a control group and an experimental group, the comparison is between distributions and not between parameters. When using nonparametric tests, we arrive at conclusions which may be valid regardless of the shape of the population values.[100]

For this reason the author did not hesitate to rely heavily on such tests, employing chi square and the Mann-Whitney U in three of the four categories of analysis. Where it was feasible, we used one parametric procedure, the difference between dependent samples or matched pairs technique, a form of t-test. We shall conclude this chapter with a brief description of the four categories of data analysis.

COMPARISONS BETWEEN EXPERIMENTAL AND CONTROL GROUPS

Six separate statistical tests were conducted in this category, four dealing with library circulation and employing the Mann-Whitney U. Circulation of all materials including mathematics was compared for the two groups over the pretest, test period, and post-test, while circulation of mathematics materials was compared only for the test period. (During the pretest and post-test, the circulation of mathematics materials was so slight as to preclude the necessity for statistical tests.) The two remaining tests involved a comparison during the test period first of the number of users of any materials including mathematics, and, second, of the number of users of mathematics materials. These tests employed the chi square technique. Again it was not necessary to use statistical tests to compare the number of users during the pretest and post-test.

COMPARISONS BETWEEN PERIODS OF EXPERIMENTAL GROUP MEDIA CENTER USE

We conducted four more statistical tests in this category which was limited to members of the experimental group and compared the library use over the three periods. These were:

1. Pretest versus test period in total circulation
2. Pretest versus test period in mathematics circulation
3. Test period versus post-test in total circulation
4. Test period versus post-test in mathematics circulation.

Here, the more rigorous parametric test of significance was employed due to the suitability of the matched pairs test. Since it is true that the data were by their nature interval rather than ordinal, we felt that a parametric statistic might well be employed to make use of this aspect. This is not to say that the rank order capabilities of the nonparametric tests are not applicable, but in the case of comparisons of the same group over different periods, the matched pairs technique is especially useful. Had the length of the three periods been equal, it would have been possible to use raw circulation figures in comparing the performance of the individual pupil over the three periods with this technique. Since the test period was of longer duration, however, the mean weekly circulation rate for each pupil was used for each of the three periods.

TYPES OF MATERIALS CIRCULATED

Only one statistical test was used in this category, a one-sample chi square test comparing the circulation by members of the experimental group of the five different types of mathematics materials. Books categorized by content (concept development, history-background, and recreational), film materials, and periodicals were compared in terms of their proportional representation on the bibliographies and their use by pupils.

The analysis included the use of various materials by all three groups over the three periods and for the most part employed percentage figures. We arrived at our conclusions on this basis together with the pupils' responses to the interview questions concerning their opinions of books as opposed to film.

CAUSALITY

The final category of data analysis concerns again our interpretation of the phenomenon of causality, and necessitated a variety of techniques in its expression. The results of the interview we analyzed carefully in building a case for teacher influence as the causal element. Results of the rating scale were similarly employed and comparisons were made using Kendall's tau (*see* Appendix H) to show the degree of association or correlation between the use of books and possible causal factors. Correlations were tested between circulation rate and the teacher's rating by pupils or the influence factor (the researcher's choice as the real cause), circulation rate and the pupils' subject interest, and circulation rate and pupils' satisfaction with materials. Also, we examined the relationship between subject interest and teacher rating in order to see if the association was as close as we expected. Finally, we analyzed the effects of the different ploys used by the teacher in motivating students to read, identifying three different levels of personal involvement on his part and revealing the success of each.

Notes

1. Ronald David Blazek, "Teacher Utilization of Nonrequired Library Materials in Mathematics and the Effect on Pupil Use" (Unpublished Ph.D. dissertation, Univ. of Illinois, 1971).

2. Saad Mohammed el-Hagrasy, "The Teacher's Role in Library Service" (Unpublished Ph.D. dissertation, Rutgers Univ., 1961), pp. 8–13.

3. Arvil S. Barr, "The Measurement and Prediction of Teaching Efficiency: A Summary of Investigations," *Journal of Experimental Education* 16:203–83 (June 1948).

4. Simon Domas and D. V. Tiedman, "Teacher Competence: An Annotated Bibliography," *Journal of Experimental Education* 19:101–218 (Dec. 1950).

5. William M. Davidson, "How to Measure the Efficiency of Teachers," in *Addresses and Proceedings of the National Education Association* (Washington, DC: National Education Assn. 51:286–90, 1913.

6. Maurice F. Freehill, "The Prediction of Teaching Competence," *Journal of Experimental Education* 31:311 (Mar. 1963).

7. Grace E. Bird, "Pupils' Estimates of Teachers," *Journal of Educational Psychology* 8:35–40 (Jan. 1917).

8. E. E. Samuelson, "The Evaluation of Teachers and Teaching," *School Executive* 60:15–16+ (May 1941).

9. H. R. Albert, "An Analysis of Teacher Rating by Pupils in San Antonio, Texas," *Educational Administration and Supervision* 27:267–74 (Apr. 1941).

10. Harry Levin, Thomas L. Hilton, and Gloria F. Leiderman, "Studies of Teacher Behavior," *Journal of Experimental Education* 26:81–91 (Sept. 1957).

11. Morris L. Cogan, "The Relation of the Behavior of Teachers to the Productive Behavior of Their Pupils" (Unpublished Ed.D. dissertation, Harvard Univ., 1954).

12. _____, "The Behavior of Teachers and the Productive Behavior of Their Pupils: I. Perception Analysis," *Journal of Experimental Education* 27:90 (Dec. 1958).

13. Levin, Hilton, Leiderman, "Teacher Behavior," p. 82.

14. Donald M. Medley and Harold E. Mitzel, "Some Behavioral Correlates of Teacher Effectiveness," *Journal of Educational Psychology* 50:239–46 (Dec. 1959).

15. Helen H. Davidson and Gerhard Lang, "Children's Perceptions of Their Teachers' Feelings toward Them Related to Self-Perception, School Achievement, and Behavior," *Journal of Experimental Education* 29:116 (Dec. 1960).

16. David L. Cole, "The Prediction of Teaching Performance," *Journal of Educational Research* 54:345–48 (May 1961).

17. Daniel Salomon, William E. Bezdek, and Larry Rosenberg, "Dimensions of Teacher Behavior," *Journal of Experimental Education* 33:23 (Fall 1964).

18. Ned A. Flanders, *Teacher Influence, Pupil Attitudes, and Achievement* (Cooperative Research Monograph no. 12; Washington, DC: Govt. Print. Off., 1965).

19. Volney A. Faw, "A Psychotherapeutic Method of Teaching Psychology," *The American Psychologist* 4:104–9 (Apr. 1949).

20. Edmund Amidon and Ned A. Flanders, "The Effects of Direct and Indirect Teacher Influence on Dependent-Prone Students in Learning Geometry," *Journal of Educational Psychology* 52:286–91 (Dec. 1961).

21. James R. Replogle, "The Relation of Teacher-Pupil Profile Pattern Similarities on Measures by Interest and Personality to Grades and Perceived Compatibility" (Unpublished Ed.D. dissertation, Lehigh Univ., 1968).

22. Goulding E. Sanderson and Kenneth E. Anderson, "A Study of the Influence of an Inspirational Science or Mathematics Teacher upon Student Achievement as Measured by the National Merit Scholarship Qualifying Test," *School Science and Mathematics* 60:346 (May 1960).

23. Weston A. Bousfield, "Students Ratings of Qualities Considered Desirable in College Professors," *School and Society* 51:253–56 (Feb. 24, 1940).

24. Edna E. Lamson, "Some College Students Describe the Desirable College Teacher," *School and Society* 56:615 (Dec. 19, 1942).

25. Arvil S. Barr, "Wisconsin Studies of the Measurement and Prediction of Teacher Effectiveness: A Summary of Investigations," *Journal of Experimental Education* 30:14–15 (Sept. 1961).

26. Archie L. Peronto, "Abilities and Patterns of Behaviors of Good and Bad Teachers" (Unpublished Ph.D. dissertation, Univ. of Wisconsin, 1942).

27. A. C. Hellfritzsch, "A Factor Analysis of Teacher Abilities," *Journal of Experimental Education* 14:166–99 (Dec. 1945).

28. Harold H. Punke, "Pupil-Teacher Relationships of High School Seniors," *Bulletin of the National Association of Secondary School Principals* 45:70 (May 1961).

29. Ibid., p. 71.

30. Ibid., p. 67.

71

31. Wilbur Brookover, "The Relation of Social Factors to Teaching Ability," *Journal of Experimental Education* 13:191–205 (June 1945).

32. R. E. Gotham, "Personality and Teaching Efficiency," *Journal of Experimental Education* 14:157–65 (Dec. 1945).

33. Donald M. Johnson and Henry C. Smith, "Democratic Leadership in the College Classroom," in *Psychological Monographs* (v. 67, no. 11; Menasha, Wis.: American Psychological Assn., 1953).

34. J. D. Krumboltz and William W. Farquhar, "The Effects of Three Teaching Methods on Achievement and Motivational Outcomes in a How-to-Study Course," in *Psychological Monographs* (v. 71, no. 14; Washington, DC: American Psychological Assn., 1957).

35. L. G. Wispe, "Evaluating Section Teaching Methods in the Introductory Course," *Journal of Educational Research* 45:161–86 (Nov. 1951).

36. W. J. McKeachie, "Motivation, Teaching Methods, and College Learning," in Marshall R. Jones, ed., *Nebraska Symposium on Motivation* (Lincoln, Neb.: Univ. of Nebraska Pr., 1961), pp. 111–42.

37. Jerome S. Bruner, *The Process of Education* (Cambridge, Mass.: Harvard Univ. Pr., 1960).

38. Lee Campion, "The Cross-Media Approach to Teaching," *High School Journal* 44:91 (Nov. 1960).

39. Robert M. W. Travers, "The Transmission of Information to Human Receivers," *Audio-Visual Communication Review* 12:373–85 (Winter 1964).

40. Frederic R. Hartz and Richard T. Samuelson, "Origin, Development, and Present State of the Secondary School Library as a Materials Center," *Peabody Journal of Education* 42:36 (July 1965).

41. Harold B. Gores, "Effective Teaching: The Role of New Educational Media," *Educational Record* 46:421–23 (Fall 1965).

42. "The Philosophy of School Libraries as Instructional Materials Centers," *Bulletin of the National Association of Secondary School Principals* 43:110–12 (Nov. 1959).

43. "New Providence Came through Its Break with Tradition in Fine Shape," *American School Board Journal* 156:17–20 (Dec. 1968).

44. Burton M. Nygren, "Student Self-Directed Study Centers," *Minnesota Journal of Education* 49:20 (Sept. 1968).

45. Sara Srygley, "A New Look at the Older Media: Printed Instructional Materials," *Bulletin of the National Association of Secondary School Principals* 50:26 (Jan. 1966).

46. Elenora Alexander, "The Librarian's Multi-Media Role," *Instructor* 74:55 (Nov. 1964).

47. "More Teaching Materials for Schools," *School and Society* 96:230 (Apr. 13, 1968).

48. Evelyn Clement, "Organization and Administration of Multi-Media Resources," *Wilson Library Bulletin* 43:360–62 (Dec. 1968).

49. Albert J. Miller, "Education in Depth Through the Learning Center," *Pennsylvania School Journal* 115:401 (Apr. 1967).

50. O. L. Davis, "Textbooks and Other Printed Materials," *Review of Educational Research* 32:127–40 (Apr. 1962).

51. Sumitra Bhargava, "An Analysis and Comparison of the Scope and Sequence of the Computational Programs in Selected Arithmetic Textbooks" (Unpublished Ph.D. dissertation, Syracuse Univ., 1956).

52. Carl Mauro, "A Survey of the Presentation of Certain Topics in Ten Series of Arithmetic Textbooks" (Unpublished Ed.D. dissertation, Univ. of Maryland, 1957).

53. Marjorie Causey, "A Comparative Study of Reading Growth: Enriched Versus Limited Program of Instruction" (Unpublished Ed.D. dissertation, Indiana Univ., 1957).

54. Frederick W. Schneider, "An Experimental Study Comparing the Effects of the Multiple Textbook Approach and the Single Textbook Approach to Elementary School Social Studies" (Unpublished Ed.D. dissertation, Univ. of Colorado, 1957).

55. Walter Hill, "Content Textbook: Help or Hindrance?" *Journal of Reading* 10:412 (Mar. 1967).

56. Nicholas C. Polos, "Textbooks—What's Wrong With Them?" *Clearing House* 38:454 (Apr. 1964).

57. Phillip W. Jackson, *The Teacher and the Machine.* (Pittsburgh: Univ. of Pittsburgh Pr., 1968).

58. George G. Dey, "A Kind Word for the Textbook," *Peabody Journal of Education* 42:241–42 (Jan. 1965).

59. Daniel Roselle, "In Defense of Good Textbooks," *Peabody Journal of Education* 44:88–90 (Sept. 1966).

60. Louise M. Berman, "In Defense of the Textbook," *Elementary English* 41:434–39 (Apr. 1964); Sam Soghomonian, "The Textbook—Tarnished Tool for Teachers," *Phi Delta Kappan* 48:395–96 (Apr. 1967); Howard F. Phillips, "A Different Approach to Textbooks," *Clearing House* 39:529 (May 1965).

61. Jerome S. Bruner, "Revolution in the Concept of a Book," *Publishers Weekly* 181:12 (Apr. 30, 1962).

62. George T. Wilkins, "The Role of Instructional Materials," *Audio-Visual Instruction* 7:704 (Dec. 1962).

63. Ralph A. Brown, "Tradebooks," *The Reading Teacher* 17:422 (Mar. 1964).

64. Paul C. Burns and Donald J. Dessart, "A Summary of Investigations Relating to Mathematics in Secondary Education: 1964," *School Science and Mathematics* 66:73–80 (Jan. 1966).

65. National Education Assn., Research Div., *The Secondary-School Teacher and Library Services* (Research Monograph 1958-M1; Washington, DC: The Association, 1958).

66. Evelyn S. Bianchi, "A Study of the Secondary-School Library and the Classroom Teacher," *Bulletin of the National Association of Secondary School Principals* 43:126 (Nov. 1959).

67. Cogan, "The Behavior of Teachers."

68. Lloyd C. Nietling, "Using Problems to Initiate the Study of Certain Topics in Mathematics" (Unpublished Ph.D. dissertation, Ohio State Univ., 1968).

69. Eugenia Schmitz, "A Study of the Library Book Collections in Mathematics and the Physical Sciences in 54 Michigan High Schools Accredited by the North Central Association of Colleges and Secondary Schools" (Unpublished Ph.D. dissertation, Univ. of Michigan, 1966).

70. Edna B. Mack, "The School Library's Contribution to the Total Educational Program of the School: A Content Analysis of Selected Periodicals in the Field of Education" (Unpublished Ph.D. dissertation, Univ. of Michigan, 1957).

71. Sister Mary Victor Korb, "Positive and Negative Factors in Team Teaching," *Mathematics Teacher* 61:50–53 (Jan. 1968).

72. Albert Wilansky, "Research Program for Gifted Secondary-School Students," *Mathematics Teacher* 54:250 (Apr. 1961).

73. David R. Johnson, "Salesmanship in the Classroom," *Wisconsin Journal of Education* 96:7–8 (Mar. 1964).

74. Joseph J. Sott, "Mathematics Enrichment Through Projects," *School Science and Mathematics* 66:737–38 (Nov. 1966).

75. Richard E. Moore, "Individualized Math," *School and Community* 54:20–21 (Feb. 1968).

76. Paul M. Nemecek, "Stimulating Pupil Interest," *School Science and Mathematics* 65:47–48 (Jan. 1965).

77. Edward W. Evans, "Identifying and Providing for the Mathematically Gifted Student," *High School Journal* 50:278–84 (Feb. 1967).

78. J. P. Crosby and A. Percival, "Mathematics and the School Library," *School Librarian* 11:258 (Dec. 1962).

79. Carol J. Howitz and Thomas A. Howitz, "The Secondary School Library: A Mathematics Laboratory," *School Libraries* 17:10 (Summer 1968).

80. Albert E. Meder, "Using the Library in High School Mathematics," *School Libraries* 8:10–13 (Mar. 1959).

81. Kenneth Taylor and J. N. Sparks, "The Secondary School Mathematics Library: Its Collection and Use," *Bulletin of the National Association of Secondary School Principals* 43:140–42 (Nov. 1959).

82. Roland L. Schmidt, "Using the Library in Junior High School Mathematics Classes," *Mathematics Teacher* 56:40–42 (Jan. 1963).

83. Lola May, "Individualized Instruction in a Learning Laboratory Setting," *Arithmetic Teacher* 13:112 (Feb. 1966).

84. Sister Antone Malerick, "A New Look at Enrichment," *Mathematics Teacher* 57:349 (May 1964).

85. Doris Y. Kuhn, "The Library and Science and Mathematics," *Theory into Practice* 6:8–11 (Feb. 1967).

86. I. E. Aaron, "Reading in Mathematics," *Journal of Reading* 8:395 (May 1965).

87. Adrian L. Hess, "The Use of the Mathematics Library in Elementary and Junior High Schools," *Arithmetic Teacher* 12:353 (May 1965).

88. Robert L. Davis, "Books in the Field: Mathematics," *Wilson Library Bulletin* 42:497–509 (Jan. 1968).

89. Wallace H. Geisz, "Modern Teaching Method for Modern Mathematics," *Bulletin of the National Association of Secondary School Principals* 52:137 (Apr. 1968).

90. Frederic R. Hartz, "High School Library: A Study in Use, Misuse, and Non-Use," *Clearing House* 38:426 (Mar. 1964).

91. Louise L. Klohn, "Six Pointers for Teachers," *Junior Libraries* 5:10 (Sept. 1958).

92. Jerry L. Walker, "Changing Attitudes toward the Library and the Librarian," *American Library Association Bulletin* 61:978 (Sept. 1967).

93. Sarah A. Burbank, "The School Library, A Showcase for Teamwork," *High School Journal* 48:279–80 (Jan. 1965).

94. Martin Rossoff, *The Library in High School Teaching* (New York: Wilson, 1961).

95. Edward W. Blakeway, "Supplementing Basal Textbooks: With Particular Focus on a Helpful Method of Solution of Inequalities," *High School Journal* 50:271 (Feb. 1967).

96. Levin, Hilton, Leiderman, "Teacher Behavior," p. 82.

97. Allan L. Bernstein, "Motivations in Mathematics," *School Science and Mathematics* 64:753 (Dec. 1964).

98. Hubert M. Blalock, *Social Statistics* (2d ed.; New York: McGraw-Hill, 1972), p. 193.

99. Fred P. Barnes, *Research for the Practitioner in Education* (Washington, DC: National Education Assn., 1964), p. 76.

100. Ibid.

4

Understanding
Student Use of Media

Having set down the procedure for acquiring the data in chapter 3, we are ready to examine the results of the experiment and analyze their significance to our comprehension of student use patterns. In chapter 3 we identified four separate categories necessary for interpreting the data: (1) comparison of media center use of experimental and control groups, (2) analysis of center use by the experimental group, (3) frequency of use of different types and forms of materials, and (4) causality or the reason for student use.

The first category constitutes a comparison between experimental and control groups in their use of the media center over the three periods to determine whether a significant difference exists when teacher utilization is present and later absent from the experimental group situation. The second category concerns only the experimental group's media center use over the three periods, analyzing the significance of the change from pretest to test period and from test period to post-test. These two categories serve to test our hypothesis and are covered in part I of this chapter while the interpretation of the other two is presented in parts II and III.

I. How Did the Groups Compare?

Experimental vs. Control

The groups studied were compared on the number of media center items borrowed and on the number of users. For center circulation, the Mann-Whitney U Test was chosen to determine if differences in circulation figures between groups were significant while chi square tests were employed for number of users. In every instance the 0.05 level was used for rejection of the null hypothesis (H_0). For the test period, both total use (and users) and mathematics use (and users) are treated statistically. This was not necessary in the case of mathematics use (and users) for the other periods.

Both Mann-Whitney and chi square are described more fully in Appendix H.

THE PRETEST: MATHEMATICS MEDIA UNDISCOVERED

The pretest covered the first six weeks of school and involved no mention of books by Mr. T to either the experimental or control group. Circulation records were kept in the media center to determine the differences which existed between the groups in their use prior to the introduction of the independent variable, teacher utilization. Although no control was instituted over the third group taught by Miss M, records were kept for purposes of comparison.

Lack of mathematics awareness. The important point to be noted (although hardly a revelation to those familiar with student behavior) is that mathematics materials were not used at all. This is indicative of a situation universal in its application since borrowers of mathematics materials generally represent a very small proportion of the totality of library patrons at the secondary school level. It is also characteristic of the lack of attention given such materials by most mathematics teachers in the discharge of their instructive responsibility and, in essence, reflects the condition which inspired this study.

Other subject materials were used in healthy fashion, especially by the control group in which 14 of the 17 pupils borrowed at least one item from the media center during this period. This is 82 percent of the group and is almost equalled by the experimental group of which 13 members or 76 percent used it at least once. These are considerably high proportions of users for each group and, more important, represent a high potential for mathematics involvement in each case. Miss M's group fell somewhat behind, here, with 10 of 16 pupils, or 63 percent of the class, having made use of such media.

Amount of circulation. In comparing the number of media center items circulated, the difference is seen to be a more substantial one than was true of the number of the center's users. Members of the control group accounted for 64 of the total number of 128 items circulated by the three groups during the pretest. This is 50 percent of the total circulation and is a disproportionate figure for the group. The experimental group was the least active of the three in terms of media center use, having borrowed only 27 items, or 21 percent of the total. Miss M's group charged out 37 items, or 29 percent of the total.

The mean weekly circulation for the experimental group as a whole was 4.49 titles, or 0.26 items per pupil. This did not compare favorably to the control group figures of 10.67 items per week for the group and 0.63 items for each pupil. The membership of Miss M's group used a mean weekly total of 6.17 library items for the group as a whole and 0.36 items for each pupil.

For the experimental and control groups to reflect such a disparity in use was at first disconcerting to the author since he considered them to be relatively homogenous at the outset, the small difference in personal characteristics (which for the most part favored the control group) having been judged unlikely to produce great differences. It is here that the element of free time as a variable (free periods during the school day), described in chapter 3 as a potentially important factor, might have been considered for statistical treatment.

The question is whether the difference in circulation during this pretest was a significant one in favor of the control group. This was not the case, however, as demonstrated in the application of the Mann-Whitney Test in table 3. The ranks of individual members of both groups are shown when combined for ranking purposes, although group identity is retained.

We are able to see that the difference is not a significant one and the null hypothesis (H_0) cannot be rejected at the 0.05 level. That is, with the obtained U of 110 and groups of 17 each, there is a probability greater than 0.05 (more than 5 cases in 100) that chance alone could account for the difference in media center use between the two groups. The critical value of U for a one-tailed test at 0.05 is 96 or less, and in the case of a two-tailed test an even more distant 87 or less. Thus we are spared the necessity of examining the factor of free periods in order to explain the difference in reading performance.

One more point should be stressed concerning the superiority of the control group as a whole. This was due to the reading activity of one individual, B5, who accounted for 29 of the 64 loans. He is the type of person whose extreme score may be said to unduly influence the statistical measurements which employ the mean. Under the Mann-Whitney in this instance, however, he naturally receives the top rank of 34, but his score does not distort the total picture. The range of circulation in the control group is 29 as compared to 6 for the experimental group, but the distribution of ranks is not significantly different from one group to another.

Therefore, the pretest of six weeks in which the reading records of all three groups were maintained provided no evidence that the experimental and control groups were not homogenous. Their performance was exactly what would be expected of two randomly selected samples drawn from the same population. The lack of interest in mathematics materials on the part of students reflects the general condition which prevails in school libraries and media centers and cannot be especially surprising to those familiar with library and media center service to the young.

TABLE 3. MANN-WHITNEY U FOR CONTROL AND EXPERIMENTAL GROUPS IN TOTAL CIRCULATION FOR PRETEST

EXPERIMENTAL GROUP PUPILS	CIRCULA-TION	RANK	CONTROL GROUP PUPILS	CIRCULA-TION	RANK
B16	6	32	B5	29	34
B8	4	29	B6	8	33
G19	4	29	B4	5	31
G16	2	22	B11	4	29
G23	2	22	G26	3	26.5
G24	2	22	G2	3	26.5
G14	1	13	G27	2	22
G15	1	13	G5	2	22
B14	1	13	G6	2	22
G17	1	13	B10	2	22
G20	1	13	G8	1	13
B23	1	13	G9	1	13
G22	1	13	G12	1	13
B1	0	4	B15	1	13
G3	0	4	G10	0	4
G11	0	4	B17	0	4
B21	0	4	B3	0	4
	27	Re = 263		64	Rc = 332

$$U = n_e n_c + \frac{n_c(n_c+1)}{2} - R_c = 110$$

$p > .05$

THE TEST PERIOD: MATHEMATICS MEDIA REVEALED

For the test period of eight weeks, the teacher actively promoted the bibliographic awareness of the members of the experimental group. Bibliographies were provided which included books, periodical articles, and films or filmstrips related to classroom studies in mathematics. Mr. T professed an ardent belief in the value of such materials to the pupils, although it was made clear that the use of such materials was not required of them. Neither tests nor reports were to be given on the material, and grades in no way would be affected.

Naturally, the control group was not given this treatment and Mr. T avoided all mention of books and other materials to its membership. As before, Miss M's group was not controlled in any way, but the record of its use of the media center was maintained for purposes of comparison. We then submitted the data to statistical analysis.

Number of users—any media. During the experiment we saw a dramatic change occur in the reading activity of the experimental group as all 17 pupils or 100 percent of the group membership charged at least one item from the center. This was true of only 12 members or 71 percent of the control group, while Miss M's group also had 12 users representing a slightly higher proportion of 75 percent. The chi square test revealed to what extent the difference in number of users was significant.

Table 4 presents the results. Since the expected frequency of nonusers in each group is less than five (2.5), a correction for continuity is needed. Blalock suggests that the correction be employed whenever the expected frequencies fall below 10 in a 2 x 2 table and states that "this correction consists of either adding or subtracting 0.5 from the observed frequencies in order to reduce the magnitude of chi square."[1] With the employment of a one-tailed test, a probability of 0.026 is achieved which is sufficient to reject H_0 for purposes of this study. That is to say that the difference between groups is significant, and we are able to conclude that for the test period the experimental group sample represents a different population of media center users than does the control group.

TABLE 4. CHI SQUARE FOR CONTROL AND EXPERIMENTAL GROUP
USERS OF ANY MEDIA, INCLUDING MATHEMATICS,
FOR THE TEST PERIOD

	USERS	NONUSERS	TOTAL
Experimental group	17	0	17
Control group	12	5	17
Total	29	5	34

chi square $= 3.75$; $p < .05$; phi square $= .11$

The measure of phi square, as given by Blalock, affords us the opportunity to determine the strength of the relationship between the number of media center users and Mr. T's utilization of mathematics materials. Phi square is a simple descriptive statistic in which the formula is given as phi square $=$ chi square/N.[2] The result of 0.11 indicates that 11 percent of the variation between groups in the number of users of any and all library materials can be traced to the utilization of media center resources by the mathematics teacher. Although a relationship of low proportions, it is quite meaningful when considering the teacher's potential.

Number of users—mathematics media. We have seen that the heightened use of mathematics materials by members of the experimental group influenced to a measurable degree the total use of the media center. Much more decisive, however, was the difference between groups in the number of users of mathematics materials. What occurred was unusual and possibly unprecedented in the annals of school librarianship when almost the entire class (88% of the membership) borrowed mathematics materials in a voluntary manner.

In sharp contrast, only one member of the control group charged out a mathematics item during the test period. This is not quite 6 percent of the group and presents a picture totally different from that of the experimental group. Miss M's group did not use any mathematics materials at all. Clearly, the difference in users of mathematics materials between the experimental group and control group was highly significant, and this is represented in table 5.

TABLE 5. CHI SQUARE FOR CONTROL AND EXPERIMENTAL GROUP
USERS OF MATHEMATICS MEDIA FOR THE TEST PERIOD

	USERS	NONUSERS	TOTAL
Experimental group	15	2	17
Control group	1	16	17
Total	16	18	34

chi square $= 19.94$; $p < .001$; phi square $= .59$

Employing a one-tailed test and the correction for continuity, the extremely high chi square value of 19.94 invalidates H_0 since it is clear that the two groups are not drawn from the same population of users of mathematics materials. In less than one case in 1,000 could such differences between groups like these be attributed to chance alone. Witness the measure of the strength of the relationship between the number of users of mathematics titles and the teacher's bibliographic activity with the experimental group. The phi square of 0.59 indicates that the teacher's activity can explain 59 percent of the variation which exists between groups, an unusually high figure. Thus, we have substantiated our case for the teacher's utilization of materials related to classroom work as part of his teaching routine in terms of its positive effects on the pupils' use of those materials.

It is interesting to note that five members of the experimental group used nothing but mathematics materials from the media center during this time while only two pupils ignored mathematics materials while using other types. As we have already pointed out, the effects of mathematics (and the mathematics teacher) on the total use of the experimental group was a factor in producing the significant difference in number of users of any materials including mathematics media. Without this disposition to use mathematics titles on the part of the experimental group, there would have been only 12 library users, precisely the same number as recorded for both the control group and the group taught by Miss M.

Mathematics circulation—an extensive change. The most exciting thing about the positive result in our experiment must necessarily be its magnitude. The experimental group accounted for 99 percent of all mathematics circulation, having charged 91 of the 92 items. The mean weekly mathematics circulation for the group was 11.38, or 0.67 items per pupil. One youngster in the control group borrowed a mathematics book during the seventh week of the test period, giving the control group a representation of 1 percent of the total mathematics circulation. This is a weekly rate of 0.13 items for the group as a whole and 0.01 items per pupil. No mathematics items were loaned to Miss M's group.

Table 6 further illustrates the superiority of the experimental group membership. Pupil G15 represents an extreme score in mathematics circulation, but does not unduly influence the character of the group in a ranking test like the Mann-Whitney U. Although she received top rank of 34, it is not because of her that the groups differ significantly. Rather, it should be noted that in almost every instance the experimental group member received higher rank than did his counterpart in the control group. Equality is achieved by only two members of the latter group in line-by-line comparison of individual ranks, these two being at the tail-end of the scale. In less than one case in a thousand would such differences be caused by chance alone. Therefore, we again reject H_0 and judge that we have wrought a remarkable change in the character of the experimental group library experience.

Effect on total circulation. The change is further understood by noting the degree to which the reading pattern of the pretest has been altered. Members of the experimental group were credited with 157 loans or more than double the control group circulation figure of 76, while Miss M's group lagged far behind with 59. The mean weekly circulation rate for the experimental group as a whole was 19.63, or 1.15 items per pupil, as compared to the control group mean of 9.50 items per week, or 0.56 per pupil. Miss M's group had a mean weekly circulation of 7.38, or 0.43 items per pupil.

The great difference in circulation between individuals of the experimental and control groups was shown to be significant with the application of the Mann-Whitney U Test, indicating in this case that we are able to reject H_0 at the 0.025 level. Therefore, in fewer than 2.5 cases out of 100 would equal or larger differences between similar groups be likely to arise by chance alone. We therefore recognize the two groups indeed to be samples of different populations with respect to their tendency to use the media center for any purpose during the test period.

TABLE 6. MANN-WHITNEY U FOR CONTROL AND EXPERIMENTAL
GROUPS ON CIRCULATION IN MATHEMATICS FOR THE
TEST PERIOD

EXPERIMENTAL GROUP PUPILS	CIRCULATION	RANK	CONTROL GROUP PUPILS	CIRCULATION	RANK
G15	28	34	G12	1	21
G22	13	33	G2	0	9.5
G20	8	31.5	G27	0	9.5
G23	8	31.5	G5	0	9.5
G14	6	30	G6	0	9.5
B8	5	28	B4	0	9.5
G19	5	28	B5	0	9.5
G24	5	28	G8	0	9.5
G3	3	25	B6	0	9.5
B23	3	25	G9	0	9.5
B1	3	25	B10	0	9.5
B14	1	21	B11	0	9.5
G17	1	21	G10	0	9.5
B16	1	21	B15	0	9.5
G16	1	21	B17	0	9.5
G11	0	9.5	G26	0	9.5
B21	0	9.5	B3	0	9.5
	91	Re = 422		1	Rc = 173

$$U = nenc + \frac{ne(ne+1)}{2} - Re = 20$$

$p < .001$

The important consideration, here, is again the effect of the mathematics teacher's activity on the total reading picture, in which his influence has been clearly demonstrated. Without the mathematics titles, the total circulation for the experimental group amounted to 66 items. This does not compare favorably with the control group total of 76 and is slightly higher than the 59 loans recorded by Miss M's group. With the inclusion of mathematics titles, however, the experimental group rates significantly higher than the control group in total library use as well as mathematics use. Most assuredly, significant differences between groups in total circulation for the

83

test period is simply a function of the exceedingly large difference in the use of mathematics materials.

THE POST-TEST: MATHEMATICS MEDIA FORGOTTEN

The post-test was conducted during the six weeks following the test period and, as in the pretest, involved no mention of materials by Mr. T to either the experimental or control groups. Circulation records were maintained for all three groups for purposes of comparison once the independent variable, teacher utilization, had been withdrawn from the experimental group situation. Again, we established no controls over Miss M's group. Another remarkable change then occurred, the complete destruction of the media center habit.

Number of users. When the teacher ceased his encouragement of media center use to members of the experimental group, they promptly forgot it as an educational aid. Only one person elected to charge out a mathematics book during this time and this came as a result of an inadvertent mention of the item by Mr. T. The control group also had one mathematics user, while the pupils in Miss M's class continued to either avoid or neglect all such titles. As a result, the total picture was altered considerably and in both the experimental group and Miss M's group 12 pupils chose to use the center for some reason representing a user proportion of 71 percent and 75 percent respectively. Slightly behind was the control group with 11 users or 65 percent proportion of users. One does not need a sophisticated analysis to comprehend that the groups do not really differ at this time.

Amount of circulation. Of the total circulation figure of 195 for the post-test, the control group accounted for 75. Second was Miss M's group with 64 loans, while the experimental group was last with 56. The mean weekly circulation for the control group was 12.50, or 0.74 items, per pupil, followed by Miss M's group with a rate of 10.67 for the group, or 0.63 items, per pupil. The experimental group recorded an average of only 9.33 library charges per week, or 0.55 items per pupil, a proportion which roughly approached three-quarters of the control group's activity. Obviously, the circulation figures for the three groups have reverted to the same order of magnitude as existed during the pretest.

Difficult though this finding might be to accept, there was absolutely no disposition to use mathematics materials on the part of the experimental group membership once the teacher ceased to show interest. As we have pointed out, even the single mathematics loan resulted from an unthinking offhand remark by Mr. T of a title thought to be interesting during the last week of the period. Although the mention of this title was in the nature of a "mistake," since it was not part of the research strategy, we find in it support for our contention (much more than a visceral reaction) that the teacher is the primary inducer of media center use by pupils. The same pupil, G12, who borrowed a math book during the test period, also was the only control group member to do this during the post-test. Therefore, both the experimental and the control groups registered a weekly rate of 0.17 mathematics items, or 0.01 per pupil, while Miss M's group again recorded none.

The difference of 19 loans in favor of the control group over the experimental group in total use for the period proved to be negligible, similar to the situation existing during the pretest. In applying the Mann-Whitney U, we found the U value was not sufficient to reject the premise that the groups belonged to the same population of users during this period. The lack of carryover may be to some a rather surprising phenomenon, the performance of the experimental group having been so different from what it had been once the independent variable was withdrawn. It was downright disappointing to the author.

Summary Totals and Analysis of Experimental Group Media Center Use

Now that we have examined the data collected during each period, it remains for us to place in proper perspective the learnings thus acquired. The following section is designed to help establish this framework for the reader by means of a brief summary review. At the same time we also undertake the second and final step in the testing of our hypothesis.

This second step refers of course to our analysis of the change which took place in the behavior of the experimental group over the three periods of the study. These comparisons are covered extensively in the original report of the study,[3] which had been done in partial completion of the requirements for the doctorate, but for the purposes of this work the description has been shortened considerably. Due to its suitability, a more rigorous parametric statistical test was employed, described by Blalock[4] as the difference between dependent samples, or the matched pairs technique. This test, which is really a form of t-test, receives fuller treatment in Appendix H.

NUMBER OF USERS—ANY MEDIA

Table 7 shows the difference between groups in terms of the number of users of any media center materials (including mathematics) over the three periods covering the first 20 weeks of school. Only in the test period did significant differences exist between the experimental and control

TABLE 7. COMPARISON OF USERS OF ANY MEDIA, INCLUDING MATHEMATICS, FOR THE THREE GROUPS OVER THE THREE PERIODS

	PRETEST PERIOD			TEST PERIOD			POST-TEST PERIOD			TOTALS		
	USERS	% OF USERS	% OF USERS WITHIN GROUP	USERS	% OF USERS	% OF USERS WITHIN GROUP	USERS	% OF USERS	% OF USERS WITHIN GROUP	USERS	% OF USERS	% OF USERS WITHIN GROUP
Experimental Group	13	35%	76%	17	42%	100%	12	34%	71%	42	37%	82%
Control Group	14	38%	82%	12	29%	71%	11	32%	65%	37	33%	72%
M Group	10	27%	63%	12	29%	75%	12	34%	75%	34	30%	71%
Totals	37	100%	74%	41	100%	82%	35	100%	70%	113	100%	75%

groups, the former responding to the utilization of media by the mathematics teacher. This response by the experimental group produced an advantage over the control group of five users of any materials (including mathematics). The chi square test showed this difference to be a significant one.

The resulting effects are indeed interesting. Owing to the activity of the test period in which all of its membership used the media center, the experimental group possessed the highest percentage of library users over the three periods with 42 of a possible 51 users (17 potential users in each period). This amounts to a proportion of 82 percent within the group and 37 percent of the total number of 113 users in the three groups. The control group is next with 37 of a possible 51 users or 72 percent of the group and 33 percent of the total number of users. Miss M's group represents slightly lower proportions. The ramifications of these conditions are easily determined since we now have actual proof that one teacher operating in what is thought to be a nonlibrary discipline can markedly affect the reading patterns of individual students in that discipline to the extent that their total media center performance picture is greatly altered.

NUMBER OF USERS—MATHEMATICS MEDIA

Table 8 demonstrates differences between groups in number of users of mathematics materials. Significant differences again are shown to exist only during the test period, but in this case they are of great magnitude. Neither group had any users of mathematics materials during the pretest, and each group had one user during the post-test. Among the membership of Miss M's group, not one pupil elected to use mathematics materials at any time during the 20 weeks of the study.

We have already expressed our surprise and disappointment in the complete lack of carryover from the test period to the post-test. Once the stimulus, teacher utilization, was withdrawn there was no difference between the experimental and control groups in their disposition to use media center materials in the subject area in which such intensive bibliographic effort had been made in preceding weeks. Obviously, this condition bears analysis and is considered here in subsequent pages.

NUMBER OF LOANS—ALL MEDIA

Table 9 provides insight into the nature of the reading patterns of the three groups over the three periods. The focal point is the test period in which the experimental group was exposed to the independent variable,

87

TABLE 8. Comparison Of Users of Mathematics Media for the Three Groups Over The Three Periods

	PRETEST PERIOD			TEST PERIOD			POST-TEST PERIOD			TOTALS		
	USERS	% OF USERS	% OF USERS WITHIN GROUP	USERS	% OF USERS	% OF USERS WITHIN GROUP	USERS	% OF USERS	% OF USERS WITHIN GROUP	USERS	% OF USERS	% OF USERS WITHIN GROUP
Experimental Group	—	—	—	15	96%	88%	1	50%	6%	16	89%	31%
Control Group	—	—	—	1	4%	6%	1	50%	6%	2	11%	4%
M Group	—	—	—	—	—	—	—	—	—	—	—	—
Totals	—	—	—	16	100%	32%	2	100%	4%	18	100%	12%

teacher utilization, for a period of eight weeks. We are able to see the extraordinary activity of the experimental group, which more than doubled the circulation figures of the control group.

The relative inactivity of the experimental group during the post-test has already been described as a surprising and rather disappointing phenomenon. The lack of carryover from the intensive preoccupation with mathematics media during the test period seems to point to the need for active interest on the part of the teacher throughout the academic year. Although the experimental group circulation totals for the three periods are the highest of the groups, they are just barely so and reflect the heavy borrowing of the test period.

The sharp contrast in media center use between the groups during the test period is demonstrated graphically in figure 1. The pyramid shape of the experimental group's use pattern is due to the unusual activity of its membership during the test period. This differs markedly from the relatively stable use pattern of the other two groups. Thus, it is obvious that an extraordinary increase has occurred in the use of the media center by the experimental group during the test period, as well as an extraordinary decrease during the post-test.

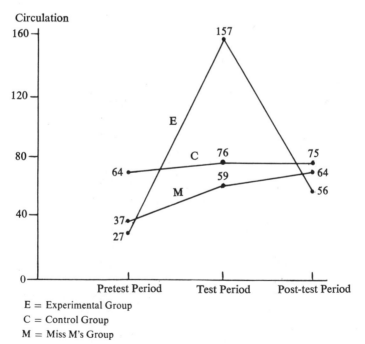

E = Experimental Group
C = Control Group
M = Miss M's Group

Figure 1. Total library circulation of the three groups over the three periods

89

TABLE 9. COMPARISON OF TOTAL CIRCULATION FOR THE THREE GROUPS OVER THE THREE PERIODS

	PRETEST PERIOD						TEST PERIOD
	CIRCU-LATION	%	MEAN WEEK-LY CIRC.	PER PUPIL MEAN WEEK-LY CIRC.	CIRCU-LATION	%	MEAN WEEK-LY CIRC.
Experimental Group	27	21%	4.50	.26	157	54%	19.63
Control Group	64	50%	10.67	.63	76	26%	9.50
M Group	37	29%	6.17	.36	59	20%	7.38
Totals	128	100%	7.11	.42	292	100%	12.17

Total use for members of this group increased nearly five-fold during the test period, and decreased nearly three-fold during the post-test. The mean increase in circulation from the pretest to the test period was over 15 items per week, or nearly one title per pupil, while the mean decrease from the test period to the post-test was over 10 items per week for the group, or more than 0.5 item per pupil. Only three pupils showed a decrease in number of media center items used from the pretest to the test period, while the remaining 14 demonstrated an increased interest in those materials. Application of the dependent samples test produces a t value of 2.996 which is significant at the 0.005 level. In plain English, we have ample proof that pupils in the experimental group exhibited a remarkable disposition to use media center materials during the test period as opposed to the pretest condition.

The picture is much the same with respect to the decrease in the use of media during the post-test. Only four pupils increased their media use during this period while the other 13 showed an expected decline. In applying the statistical test, a t of 2.030 is found which is significant at the 0.05 level but not quite at the 0.025 level. Again, we have predicted the direction of change and therefore have demonstrated a comprehension of the effect of teacher utilization, this time in its withdrawal. Total media center use for the experimental group lessened significantly when Mr. T ceased his bibliographic activity in mathematics class.

			POST-TEST PERIOD				TOTALS	
PER PUPIL MEAN WEEKLY CIRC.	CIRCULATION	%	MEAN WEEKLY CIRC.	PER PUPIL MEAN WEEKLY CIRC.	CIRCULATION	%	MEAN WEEKLY CIRC.	PER PUPIL MEAN WEEKLY CIRC.
1.15	56	29%	9.33	.55	240	39%	12.00	.71
.57	75	38%	12.50	.74	215	35%	10.75	.63
.43	64	33%	10.67	.63	160	26%	8.00	.47
.72	195	100%	10.83	.64	615	100%	10.25	.60

NUMBER OF LOANS—MATHEMATICS MEDIA

Table 10 illustrates the superiority of the experimental group over the others in the use of mathematics materials. The test period again is the central point and clearly reveals the effects of the independent variable, teacher utilization. The activity of the test period is even more striking here than was true in the case of all types of materials circulated. The literature indicates that mathematics is a neglected area of school media center activity and this we found to be true. Both the pretest and post-test show the degree to which such materials are neglected when no guidance or encouragement is provided the pupil. On the other hand, when Mr. T actively engaged in bibliographic activities, 15 of his 17 pupils increased their use of mathematics materials, while only two continued to ignore them. When the formula is applied, a t of 3.263 is realized which is the largest value obtained thus far. H_0 is again rejected at the 0.005 level, indicating that in fewer than 5 cases in 1,000 having this t value could the difference between groups be attributed to chance alone. In unmistakable fashion, we thus confirmed the validity of our premise that teacher activity can effect changes in student reading patterns without threat of punishment or promise of reward.

The mean decrease in use of mathematics items during the post-test by members of the experimental group is only slightly less than the increase recorded during the test period owing to the circulation of one mathematics book during the final week. We have pointed out that the teacher

91

TABLE 10. COMPARISON OF CIRCULATION IN MATHEMATICS FOR THE
THREE GROUPS OVER THE THREE PERIODS

	PRETEST PERIOD						TEST PERIOD
	CIRCU-LATION	%	MEAN WEEKLY CIRC.	PER PUPIL MEAN WEEKLY CIRC.	CIRCU-LATION	%	MEAN WEEKLY CIRC.
Experi-mental Group	—	—	—	—	91	99%	11.38
Control Group	—	—	—	—	1	1%	.13
M Group	—	—	—	—	—	—	—
Totals	—	—	—	—	92	100%	3.83

also was responsible for that loan having inadvertently mentioned the title in class. The two pupils who were unmoved by the teacher's bibliographic activity during the test period were consistent in their neglect of mathematics materials during the post-test. All 15 pupils who increased their use of these materials during the test period showed an expected drop during the post-test.

The surprising thing was the magnitude of the decline. This may or may not be a result of the conditioned disinterest on the part of the young media center users to mathematics resources. At the least, it represents the inability to retain as media center users mathematics pupils of this level when the teacher does not continue to actively promote the media available in this subject. This may be true with respect to the content of any subject, but is probably more characteristic of the disciplines regarded as minor media center users.

Application of our statistical test results in a t of 3.214, again significant at the 0.005 level, and indicates in characteristic fashion the importance of the elimination of the independent variable. Thus we know that when the teacher ceases to show interest in mathematics materials, there is a tendency toward complete neglect of these items on the part of the class. This phenomenon is further examined under the section dealing with the motivation of pupils.

Summary

In testing our hypothesis, we found a significant difference between the experimental and control groups in the use of media center materials dur-

	POST-TEST PERIOD						TOTALS	
PER PUPIL MEAN WEEKLY CIRC.	CIRCU-LATION	%	MEAN WEEKLY CIRC.	PER PUPIL MEAN WEEKLY CIRC.	CIRCU-LATION	%	MEAN WEEKLY CIRC.	PER PUPIL MEAN WEEKLY CIRC.
.67	1	50%	.17	.01	92	98%	4.60	.27
.01	1	50%	.17	.01	2	2%	.10	.01
—	—	—	—	—	—	—	—	—
.23	2	100%	.11	.01	94	100%	1.57	.09

ing the test period, but not during the pretest or post-test. Statistical applications showed these differences to relate not only to mathematics materials but also to total circulation. It was evident that the teacher had influenced the use of the media center by the experimental group membership, only two of whom did not use mathematics materials during the test period. The effects of the teacher's activity were clearly demonstrated by the increase in the use of such media during the test period and the decrease during the post-test.

The fact that the experimental group used mathematics materials in an extraordinary manner at the time it was receiving special treatment indicates the effectiveness of that treatment. On this basis, it is possible to state that teacher utilization does determine to a great degree the disposition of pupils to use the media center. This is true even with respect to a skills subject like mathematics which is generally overlooked in media center operations. The influence of the mathematics teacher, Mr. T, in this instance was great enough to alter completely the pattern of use common among his pupils, the experimental group doubling the control group in total use during the test period. During the pretest, the experimental group ranked behind the other two in circulation figures.

It is important to note that the effects on pupil behavior cease immediately upon termination of the teacher's bibliographic activity. We saw this when the groups in the post-test reverted to the use pattern represented in the pretest. This may very well be a reflection of conditioned behavior, i.e., the neglect of mathematics media. It appears to be a real indicator of the need for continuous bibliographic activity on the part of the mathematics teacher in order to assure the use by pupils of such materials. It possibly mirrors the need to reinforce learnings of any type at the junior high school level, especially those which seek to establish a new behavioral pattern. The lack of carryover from the test period to the post-test is at any rate an important consideration and receives more attention in subsequent pages.

II. What Materials Did They Use?

The hypothesis having been tested, it remains for us to examine the materials used and, after that, the possible causes and reasons for students following teachers' suggestions. One of the important aspects of our study, as we explained in the introductory pages, was our focus on supplementary materials and the possible inclinations of pupils to choose one medium over another or one type of book over another when given a choice. We shall analyze these considerations here.

Effect of Instruction on Choice of Medium

Table 11 gives the figures for all materials circulated over the three periods by each of the three groups and indicates proportional use of each form. We can see that the experimental group, in its use of the media center, demonstrated a tendency to select a higher proportion of nonbook material than did the others. During the pretest, eight recordings were borrowed for 30 percent of the group's total library circulation as compared to only one recording, or 2 percent of the total, for the control group and two recordings, or 5 percent, for Miss M's group. Our feeling is that this is an indication of the number of pupils enrolled in the music course (13 in the experimental group and 4 in the control group). All recordings were charged to these pupils.

Another example of the relationship of instruction to use of a certain medium is found in the test period. Only in the experimental group do we have users of film material, and such use occurred only during this period. These were mathematics filmstrips and film loops recommended by Mr. T, and the 24 loans constitute 15 percent of the total number of 157 loans for the period. Four recordings were circulated to two members of the experimental group, both of whom were taking music as was the one pupil in the control group who borrowed a recording. Four recordings were circulated to three members of the group taught by Miss M, two of whom also were enrolled in the music course. The other pupil charged a poetry recording (probably related to English study).

TABLE 11. NUMBER AND PERCENTAGE BY FORM OF ALL MEDIA, INCLUDING MATHEMATICS, BORROWED BY THE THREE GROUPS OVER THE THREE PERIODS

MEDIA	PRETEST PERIOD			TEST PERIOD			POST-TEST PERIOD			THREE-PERIOD TOTALS		
	CIRCULATION		USERS	CIRCULATION		USERS	CIRCULATION		USERS	CIRCULATION		USERS
	NUMBER	%		NUMBER	%		NUMBER	%		NUMBER	%	
Experimental Group												
Books	19	70%	10	105	67%	15	50	89%	12	174	72%	16
Recordings	8	30%	4	4	3%	2	4	7%	2	16	7%	6
Periodicals	—	—	—	24	15%	7	2	4%	1	26	11%	8
Film	—	—	—	24	15%	10	—	—	—	24	10%	10
Total	27	100%		157	100%		56	100%		240	100%	
Control Group												
Books	63	98%	14	70	92%	12	72	96%	11	205	96%	15
Recordings	1	2%	1	1	1%	1	3	4%	2	5	2%	3
Periodicals	—	—	—	5	7%	1	—	—	—	5	2%	1
Film	—	—	—	—	—	—	—	—	—	—	—	—
Total	64	100%		76	100%		75	100%		215	100%	
M Group												
Books	35	95%	9	54	91%	9	63	98%	11	152	95%	15
Recordings	2	5%	2	4	7%	3	—	—	—	6	4%	4
Periodicals	—	—	—	1	2%	1	1	2%	1	2	1%	2
Film	—	—	—	—	—	—	—	—	—	—	—	—
Total	37	100%		59	100%		64	100%		160	100%	
Three-Group Totals												
Books	117	91%	33	229	79%	36	185	94%	34	531	86%	46
Recordings	11	9%	7	9	3%	6	7	4%	4	27	4.5%	13
Periodicals	—	—	—	30	10%	9	3	2%	2	33	5.5%	11
Film	—	—	—	24	8%	10	—	—	—	24	4%	10
Total	128	100%		292	100%		195	100%		615	100%	

95

Seven members of the experimental group are credited with 24 loans of periodicals for a proportion of 15 percent of the total circulation during the test period. Ten of these charges were periodical articles in mathematics mentioned by Mr. T, while the remaining 14 loans represented a combination of periodicals and pamphlets (also included in this category), most of which appeared to be closely related to classwork in English and social studies. In the control group there were only five such charges representing 7 percent of the total of 76, and only one in Miss M's group for a proportion of 2 percent of the total circulation of 59. Again, it is our feeling that the difference favoring the experimental group in the circulation of nonbook material outside the field of mathematics is due chiefly to the different routines employed by several teachers who handled subfreshman classes in these areas.

During the post-test, members of the experimental group recorded an increase in the proportion of book use for which the 50 loans represent 89 percent of their total of 56 charges. Four recordings were circulated as during the test period, but there was no film circulation, and only two periodicals, charged to one user, were borrowed. In the control group, books continued their dominance, 11 users accounting for 72 of the 75 loans, or 96 percent of the total. Three recordings were charged to two users for the remainder of the total. Eleven pupils in Miss M's group charged 63 books of the total of 64 charges, the other loan being a periodical.

In none of the three periods did the proportion of book use in either the control group or Miss M's group fall below 91 percent, reflecting an obvious disposition on the part of the students to select books rather than nonbook material. Of the 615 items circulated by the three groups over the three periods, 531, or 86 percent, were books. These were borrowed by 46 different pupils of the total subfreshman class of 50. There were 33 charges of periodical material for a proportion of 5.5 percent which were credited to 11 pupils. Loans of recordings numbered 27, or 4.5 percent of the total; these were borrowed by 13 individuals. The only film material loaned was to the ten members of the experimental group during the test period, a circulation total of 24 which constituted 4 percent of the charges by all groups in all three periods. The implication, of course, is that without the teacher's encouragement to use nonbook material in the library, titles of this nature are neglected by pupils.

Circulation of Mathematics Media During the Test Period

Records were kept which indicate the amount of use to which each item on the weekly bibliographies was put. Naturally, it is primarily a record of the reading activity of the experimental group which received from the teacher the bibliographies and the encouragement to use them. The one instance of use by a member of the control group occurred during the seventh week, and it was of a book which appeared on the sixth week bibliography. This was a popular recreational item by Gardner, entitled *The Scientific American Book of Mathematical Puzzles and Diversions*. It was not the reserve copy that was borrowed in this instance but a duplicate from the regular collection, which probably indicates that the youngster was unaware of the experiment and simply followed her own inclinations in borrowing it.

On several occasions use was made of an item which appeared on the bibliography for a previous week. Two items were used twice in this manner, the first being a charge during the third week and also during the fourth week of a film loop, *Motion Geometry #1*, appearing on the bibliography for the second week. The other was a loan during the fifth week and also during the sixth week of a recreational book, *Fantasia Mathematica*, which appeared on the bibliography for the fourth week.

Other examples involved a filmstrip, *Angles*, which was used during the fourth week after having been introduced by the bibliography for the third week, and a historical book, *Wonderful World of Mathematics*, charged during the seventh week after appearing on the bibliography for the third week. The two remaining instances concern recreational books, *Paper Folding for the Mathematics Class*, a fifth week item used during the sixth week, and the previously mentioned book by Gardner, charged by the control group pupil.

Most titles on the bibliographies were used at least once, and in no single week were more than two items unused. During the last three weeks of the period, all titles were used, as was true also of the fourth week. The most popular items proved to be the film loop, *Motion Geometry #1*, and the recreational book, *Fantasia Mathematica*, each of which was borrowed seven times. Of the seven titles which were not used at all, four were books concerned with concept development or skill mastery, two were books of history-background type, and one was a periodical article. All films or filmstrips were used at least once, and it should be noted that the film loop *Motion Geometry #2*, appearing in the bibliography of the fifth week, was burned out and retired early in the week after being circulated four times.

Distribution by Form

Of the 92 charges credited to subfreshmen during the test period, a total of 58 were books. Of these, recreational books were charged 24 times, followed by concept development or skill mastery books with 23 loans, and finally by history-background books with 11 loans. Film material and recreational books were used each week of the test period, and periodical articles and concept development books in all but one. Books of history-background type were unused in two of the eight weeks.

Table 12 provides a better understanding of the disposition of individuals to favor certain types of materials over others. It is limited to members of the experimental group inasmuch as they alone were equipped with the weekly bibliographies and received encouragement from the teacher. Therefore, they were the only pupils provided with the full apparatus necessary in making the best decisions as to which materials to use and when. The one recreational book loaned to the youngster in the control group is disregarded here since it represents a choice made within a more limited framework.

Pupil G15 is one of the three pupils to have used all types of materials as well as the only one to use something each week of the test period. Her total of 28 charges is highest for the group, followed by pupil G22 with 13. All the other pupils borrowed less than 10 items each. Two pupils did not charge out any titles at all while four others borrowed only one item each. All 10 users of film material were also users of books, except for pupil B16 whose one film charge was his only loan.

THE GENERAL PREFERENCE FOR FILM AND RECREATIONAL BOOKS

Although concept development or skill mastery books had the most users, 11 pupils who accounted for 23 loans, one must remember that there were twice as many items of this type in the bibliographies. Therefore, recreational books and film material, each with 10 users credited with 23 and 24 charges respectively, ranked much higher in proportional use. There were seven users of history-background books with a circulation of 11; while periodical articles were least favored with six users accounting for 10 loans.

Comparing the weekly circulation rate per title of the different types of media, we are able to see that the use of history-background books, concept development books, and periodicals is approximately the same over the eight weeks. This is also true of recreational books and film material, except at a level of use more than twice as much in proportion to the others. The remarkable feature here is that the films used were actually concept development material, if we were to analyze them by content. Thus, students used concept development film material about twice as frequently on the average as they did books of similar content. In fact, use of film

TABLE 12. Types of Mathematics Media Borrowed by Individual Members of the Experimental Group During the Test Period

PUPILS	TYPES OF MEDIA CIRCULATED EACH WEEK								CIRCULATION BY TYPE OF MEDIA					
	WEEK													
	1	2	3	4	5	6	7	8	c	h	r	f	p	TOTAL
B1					r		h	h	–	2	1	–	–	3
G3							rch		–	1	1	–	–	3
B8		fh	c		rc				2	1	1	1	–	5
G11									–	–	–	–	–	
G14	rfp				crf				1	–	2	2	1	6
G15	rfp	rfp	rfph	rrfpc	cf	chrf	ccf	crfp	6	2	7	8	5	28
B14	c								1	–	–	–	–	1
G16	c								1	–	–	–	–	1
G17				f					–	–	–	1	–	1
B16				c					1	–	–	–	–	1
G19		f	f			rr	p		–	–	2	2	1	5
G20	f	f			f	f	f	ccp	2	–	–	5	1	8
B23				rf	r				–	–	2	1	–	3
G22				chrf		chfp	chr	cr	4	3	3	2	1	13
B21									–	–	–	–	–	
G23					cr	cfp	chr		3	1	2	1	1	8
G24				r	crf	h			1	1	2	1	–	5
									23	11	23	24	10	91
Weekly Circulation Rate									1.4	1.4	2.9	3.0	1.3	1.9

c = concept development books (skill mastery)
h = history-background books
r = recreational books
f = film material
p = periodicals

99

most nearly approximated the use of recreational books, which may well be an indication of the manner in which pupils tend to view the medium.

If students consider film to be enjoyable or less taxing mentally, this would explain their preference for this medium when given a choice. The periodical articles were of varied content; none received an unusual amount of use. The only article not used at all was "Symmetry in Nature," which was primarily a piece of background information; however, it also possesses an element of concept mastery and that may account for its lack of use. The other articles each were borrowed either once or twice per week. If all types of books are considered together as the form of a medium and the use of the three types (concept, history-background, and recreational) is averaged, a mean use per title of 1.9 per week is found. This is precisely the weekly rate of circulation of all the media when taken together. The data indicate that books were used more frequently on the average than were periodical articles, but less frequently than film material.

Table 13 shows the disproportionate use of recreational books and film as compared to the other classes of materials in terms of percentages for which column 6 is most meaningful. The use of film exceeded by 10.3 percent its proportional representation in the mathematics bibliographies, while the use of recreational books surpassed its presence in numbers by 8.3 percent. The other three classes of materials fell below their proportionate numbers: concept development books by 8.3 percent, periodical articles by 5.7 percent, and history-background books by 4.7 percent. If books are considered together as a form, the total of the three types results in a

TABLE 13. NUMBER AND PERCENTAGE OF MATHEMATICS MEDIA LOANS MADE BY THE EXPERIMENTAL GROUP DURING THE TEST PERIOD

TYPES OF MEDIA	NO. OF TITLES	CIRCU- LATION	PERCENT OF USE	PERCENT OF TITLES	DIFFERENCE
Books					
c	16	23	25%	33.3%	−8.3%
h	8	11	12%	16.7%	−4.7%
r	8	23	25%	16.7%	8.3%
Film	8	24	27%	16.7%	10.3%
Periodical articles	8	10	11%	16.7%	−5.7%
Totals	48	91	100%	100%	

c = concept development (skill mastery)
h = history-background
r = recreational

use proportion of 62 percent as compared to a proportional representation in the bibliographies of 66.7 percent. The use of books, then, falls below the expected figure by 4.7 percent.

We applied the chi square test to determine whether or not such differences could be considered significant, and found that the chi square of 13.83 is significant at the 0.05 level which has been chosen for rejection of H_0, and is in fact significant at the 0.01 level. In this case, H_0 states that the distribution of circulation among the five types of materials is no different than what may be expected as a result of chance alone in any normal situation. We reject this premise thoroughly and acknowledge that the disproportionate average use of recreational books and film material is not a chance factor. Whether or not the use of such items can be associated in terms of the pupils' view of film as a recreational medium is an interesting and important point; it is examined further in the section on student interviews. One should remember, however, the actual circulation of concept development books did equal that of recreational books, and fell only one short of equalling the number of film loans.

SUMMARY

We have seen that a significant difference exists in the use of certain classes of mathematics media on the part of the experimental group with respect to proportionate number of titles on the bibliographies. Making their selection from a weekly bibliography of six items, the pupils favored recreational books and film materials over concept development books, history-background books, and periodical articles. The important point is that youngsters may tend to consider the projected image as recreational or less demanding than are books, and will, when given a choice by the teacher, choose the more desirable means of fulfilling an obligation or performing a duty. This amounts to following the path of least effort and resistance, a decidedly human characteristic.

In treating all types of books together as a form, we have seen that the medium was used to a greater degree proportionally than was the periodical article, but to a lesser degree than was the film. This contrasts strongly with the use of media center materials by all groups over the three periods in which books were an overwhelming choice of the users. Even in the experimental group, the incidence of book use as compared to that of other media increased during the post-test. Thus we have support for our belief that to make these pupils users of such materials in the media center, a teacher must take continued initiative. There is also something to be said for the form in which substantive information is presented and the effect on voluntary use by pupils, which is further examined in the following pages.

101

III. Interview and Rating Scale Results

After the test period had ended, an interview was held with every member of the experimental and control groups. The interviewing was done during the Christmas vacation in the respondent's own home. The primary purpose of interviewing the experimental group membership was to examine the nature of causality. It was hoped that the examination of the phenomena through question 3 (*see* Appendix E) would turn up evidence in favor of our premise that teacher influence rather than any other single factor led to the pupils' use of the materials. Also important is our concern for another possible causal element: pupils' satisfaction with library materials is approached through questions 4, 5, and 7 of the interview schedule. Questions 1 and 2 deal with causality in a more general way.

The control group was interviewed primarily to make the students aware of the existence and availability of the mathematics items. This was, in effect, a partial control on another possible causal factor, guidance. Only one question to this group as a whole concerned causality, and that was question 5 of the interview schedule (*see* Appendix F). The one pupil, G12, who borrowed a mathematics book was given the same line of questions as were the users in the experimental group.

The second important consideration in structuring the interview was the focus on the pupils' preferences for either book or film. The nature of the pupils' inclination to use one type of material over another is examined by questions 8, 9, and 10 of the experimental group interviews, and by questions 7 and 8 of the control group interviews.

The rating scale (Appendix D) was used to gauge the pupils' feelings about the teacher as an indicator of teacher influence, and to determine their interest in mathematics. We expected similarities between the two groups in their value judgments on these points. Taking the rating scale and the interviewing together, we should have enough information to provide an analysis of the potential causes of student use of the media center. Tables 14 and 15 show the results of the interview with members of both groups.

Interview Questions of a General Nature

EXPERIMENTAL GROUP

Only one question of a general nature was included in the interview schedule for this group, and that was a check on the validity of the reading record for each pupil who was designated a user of mathematics material. Of the 15 pupils regarded as users, 10 identified a title correctly and ac-

TABLE 14. EXPERIMENTAL GROUP INTERVIEW RESPONSES

RESPONSE	NUMBER OF RESPONDENTS	PUPILS
1. The teacher spent so much time talking about books because		
He wanted us to learn new information and get different ideas on our own and to get a better understanding of the topics	15	All except G11 & B16
He wanted us to develop an interest in and enjoyment of math	2	G11, B16
2. He was right because		
The teacher should tell us about such materials since he can't cover everything in class	8	G11, G14, G20, G22, G24, B8, B14, B23
Pupils do get additional information from outside reading	7	G3, G15, G17, G19, B1, B16, B21
He was wrong because it took up too much time	1	G23
I am undecided because it didn't make much difference to me	1	G16
3a. I used math materials more than once because		
I wanted to show the teacher that I was interested	7	G14, G15, G20, G24, G19, G22, B8
I wanted to get more information and help	2	B23, G23
Some of them were interesting	1	B1
3b. I used math materials on only one occasion because		
I did not have much time	4	G3, G16, G17, B14
I didn't want to spend much time on nonrequired work	1	B16
3c. I used no math materials because I don't generally follow optional recommendations	2	B21, G11
4. I was satisfied with the library materials because they were interesting and helpful	6	G15, G16, G17, G19, G24, B14
I was not entirely satisfied because		
Some titles were less interesting than others	6	G14, G20, G22, B1, B8, B23
The one title I used was somewhat difficult and dull	1	B16
I was disappointed because they were not interesting	2	G3, G23
5. I was always able to get the titles I wanted from the library	8	B1, G14, G16, G17, G19, G20, G22, G24
I was not always able to get the titles I wanted from the library	7	B16, B23, G3, G15, G23, B8, B14
6. I can tell you about a title I read	10	·G16, G19, G20, G22, G23, G24, B1, B8, B14, B23
Identified title correctly and described content		
Couldn't remember title but described content	5	G3, G14, G15, G17, B16

TABLE 14. (CONTINUED)

RESPONSE	NUMBER OF RESPONDENTS	PUPILS
7. Math materials are enjoyable for me	13	All except G3, G11, G20, B16
The materials are not enjoyable because they are not entertaining	4	G3, G11, G20, B16
Math materials are helpful to me in achieving a grade	4	G15, G17, G24, B8
They are not helpful because		
Test material is not included in content	10	G3, G16, G20, G22, G23, G14, G19, B14, B16, B23
I don't need them	3	G11, B1, B21
8. I used filmstrips because		
I thought it would be easier and more interesting than books	7	G15, G19, G20, G22, G23, B8, B16
Mr. T made special mention of the film loop	3	G14, G24, B3
I didn't use film or filmstrip because		
I think about books first	3	G16, G17, B1
The film loop was burned out when I asked for it	2	G3, B14
The same reasons I didn't use books	2	G11, B21
9. Books are more important in math but film should also be used (books are more comprehensive)	9	G3, G11, G14, G15, G17, G24, B8, B21, B23
Books and filmstrips are equally important in math because		
Film complements books and can focus on certain concepts with pictures	6	G16, G19, G23, G20, B1, B16
Film is especially helpful in motion geometry and can hold interest	1	B14
Change in routine is needed	1	G22
10. Books are more important in history but both should be used	4	G16, G17, B8, B21
Both are important in an equal sense in history because		
Books are more comprehensive but pictures are more helpful in explaining the social conditions		All except G16, G17, B8, B21
Books are more important in English but both should be used because		
Books are more detailed but film can help clarify concepts in grammar	7	G3, G15, G16, G19, B1, B16, B23
Movies of plays or novels are interesting	1	G20
Films are of no use in English because		
They are ineffective	4	G14, G11, G22, B8
I cannot imagine a use for them	5	G24, G23, G17, B14, B21

TABLE 15. CONTROL GROUP INTERVIEW RESPONSES

RESPONSE	NUMBER OF RESPONDENTS	PUPILS
1. I remember library orientation for sub-freshmen	15	all except G26, B24
I didn't attend it since I am a freshman	2	G26, B24
2. I recall my math teacher saying that books would be placed on reserve	3	B5, B10, B17
I don't recall it	14	all except B5, B10, B17
3. I didn't know that math books were on reserve	16	all except G27
I did know	1	G27
4a. I knew about them because one of the people in the other class mentioned it. Since Mr. T didn't mention it to us, I didn't do anything about it	1	G27
4b. Nobody in Mr. T's other class discussed it	14	all except G27, G8, G5
One of the students in the other class said that they were reading books but since Mr. T didn't ask us to do it, I didn't look for them	2	G8, G5
5. I didn't use library materials in mathematics more often because I don't think about math books when I go to the library	16	all except G12
I did use a math book but I haven't been going to the library much	1	G12
6. I feel that math materials can be enjoyable	15	all except G6, B24
Math materials are not enjoyable	2	G6, B24
Math materials can be helpful in clarifying concepts	16	all except B4
Math materials are not helpful since they probably wouldn't cover the work done in class	1	B4
7. Books are more important in math but both books and films should be used	9	G2, B4, B10, G10, G5, B5, B6, B11, B24
Books and filmstrips are equally important	5	B15, B17, G8, G9, G27
Filmstrips are more important than books but both should be used since concepts are better explained by pictures	3	G6, G12, G26
8. Books are more important in history but both should be used	8	G2, G6, G27, B4, B6, B11, B15, G9
Filmstrips are more important than books because they show better how people lived and books are more difficult	2	B5, G26
Books and filmstrips are equally important	7	G5, G8, G10, G12, B10, B17, B24

TABLE 15. (CONTINUED)

RESPONSE	NUMBER OF RESPONDENTS	PUPILS
Books are more important in English but both should be used	8	G26, B11, B6, G8, B15, B17, B10, G27
Films are not at all useful in English	9	B5, B24, G9, G6, B4, G10, G5, G12, G2

Questions about mathematics materials for G12* only:
6a. I found the math book by just browsing in   1
the 500s section
From Experimental Group Interview Schedule
4. I was satisfied because I like the challenges
5. I was always successful in getting the math
materials I wanted
6. I can tell you about the book (she
identified and described correctly)
8. I didn't use film since I didn't think about
it and the teacher didn't mention them

*Only Control Group member to borrow a mathematics book from the media center during the study.

curately described its content. Five users could not remember any titles they had borrowed but accurately described the content of an item on the bibliography. Each of the 15 pupils apparently had read at least one item and by the definition employed in chapter 1 fit into our category of media center user.

CONTROL GROUP

The first four questions for the control group were of a general nature and revealed some interesting although not surprising information. Responses to question 1 indicate that all members of the group who were exposed to the week-long library orientation period remembered it, but responses to question 2 show that the teacher's fleeting mention of library materials some nine or ten weeks earlier had been forgotten by 14 of the 17 pupils. The answers to questions 3 and 4 show that three of the pupils in the group knew of the use of materials by the experimental group but did not feel inclined to use them simply because the teacher did not mention it to them. Somewhat surprising is our success in concealing the use of media by the experimental group from the majority of the control group membership. The prevailing sentiment was that, although they talk among themselves about the personal qualities of teachers, students seldom mention teaching routines unless they are extraordinary in some sense. Apparently the utilization of mathematics media was not extraordinary.

Interview Questions about Media Preferences

EXPERIMENTAL GROUP

Responses to question 8 show that of the ten users of film material, seven used it because they felt that such items would be easier or more interesting than books. This group included pupil G20 who charged five films as opposed to two books and pupil G16 whose only loan was of this nature. This supports our belief that film may be viewed as a recreational medium by pupils. The other users stated that the teacher's special emphasis on the film loop (in which he discussed the operation of the equipment as well as its value) led them to use it. Three pupils thought primarily about books when in the media center and were not inclined to use film, while two potential users were disappointed in their request because the film loop had burned. The two nonusers of mathematics material felt a general reluctance to do optional work of any kind.

In response to question 9, nine pupils felt that books were more important in mathematics due to the amount of detail in one volume as opposed to a whole series of film, although both media were of value. Eight pupils felt that film material was equally important primarily because of the capacity to present concepts through pictures. The 10 pupils who used film were equally divided on this point. The heaviest user of film material was pupil G15 (also the heaviest user of books and periodicals), and it was her opinion that books were of primary importance. The two nonusers were in agreement on this point.

Question 10 reveals that 13 pupils felt that books and film are of equal value in the study of history, balancing the comprehensiveness of books with the capacity of film to depict the social condition of a time or place. Except for pupil G16, the four individuals who felt that books were somewhat more important in history were of similar mind in mathematics. Film was considered to be of least value in the study of English for which nine pupils felt that there was no need to employ the medium. Of these nine, six had stated a preference for the use of books in mathematics (pupils G11, G14, G24, G17, B8, and B21). The last three also favored books over film in history. This group of six included three pupils who had used film in mathematics (G14, G24, and B8), as well as pupil B21 who had not used any mathematics materials. Eight pupils felt that although books are more important in English, film should also be used.

CONTROL GROUP

In this group, there were several individuals who were more emphatic in their expression of favor regarding the value of film in mathematics. Three pupils stated that film material is more important in mathematics than are books, the facility inherent in the pictorial development of concepts outweighing the value found in the comprehensiveness of the single book. Nine pupils in their response to question 7 indicated that books are more important but film should also be used. This was the same number who were of this opinion in the experimental group. The remaining five pupils felt that the two media are of equal importance. The responses to question 8 indicate that this group is somewhat more reserved about the probable value of film in the study of history inasmuch as only seven members felt that film was of equal value to books as compared to 13 in the experimental group. Eight members of the control group felt that books are of greater value, whereas only four members of the experimental group felt this way. Again, however, there are two responses which favor film over books and cite the boring nature of books as opposed to the more interesting view of the social condition provided by film. One of these respondents (G26) was of similar mind with respect to mathematics materials.

The reaction to the two media in the study of English is exactly the same as that of the experimental group. Nine pupils were of the opinion that film was not at all useful to the study of English for the same reasons expressed by the other group. Included in this category are three of the four individuals who considered film material more important than books in either mathematics or history. Only pupil G26 of this group of four joined with seven others in the feeling that although books are more important, both media should be used.

SUMMARY

That books are considered to be of primary importance by members of the experimental group is most clearly expressed with respect to the study of English where pupils showed relatively little interest in the use of film material due to the ineffectiveness of materials they have seen or to their lack of exposure to such materials in the subject. Although no pupil in this group was willing to concede that film material may be of greater value in any subject than are books, 13 felt that the medium was of equal value in the study of history. Eight pupils felt that this was also true of mathematics. The membership of the control group had feelings similar with respect to the relative importance of the two media, except that four individuals felt that film was superior to books in either mathematics or history. The lack of interest in film as a suitable medium for the study of English was present.

Most important, here, we have a rather clearly drawn picture of student sentiment regarding mathematics film material. Responses to question 8 of the experimental group interview indicate that seven of the 10 users said they used it because they felt it to be easier or more interesting than books. This supports our contention that the disproportionate average use of film during the test period was related to the view that such material is less taxing mentally and more enjoyable. When taken together with the fact that the use of media center materials was not a required task, the pupils' line of reasoning is completely comprehensible. To fulfill the desires of an influential teacher, the path of least effort involved the use of film. Needless to say this has tremendous ramifications for the use of such material in a meaningful way.

The Nature of Causality or the Irrepressible Why

Earlier, we identified certain possible causes for the pupils' disposition to use library materials in mathematics in a voluntary manner. Most important in our estimation was the factor of teacher influence, or the ability of the teacher to effect changes in the school-related activity of his pupils. This is the explanation we favored, while at the same time we were cognizant of the potential value of bibliographic guidance or the provision of annotated lists which focused on relevant topics and explained the reason for the inclusion of each item. For our purposes, we have chosen to include guidance within the broad fabric of teacher influence, although we shall discuss it as a separate factor.

TEACHER INFLUENCE AS A FACTOR

Teacher influence we considered to be of primary importance, and it therefore represents the causal element in our hypothesis. A survey of the literature of the field of teacher behavior and teacher effectiveness found two characteristics recognized consistently as being important to pupils in their evaluation of the teacher. Most germane was the teacher's personality and next his or her expertise as an instructor. We adopted the premise that the key to the amount of influence wielded by a teacher resides in the assessment by the pupils of his personality and ability. Thus developed our line of reasoning in which either or both of these aspects were considered to be the stimulus for the pupils' voluntary reading activity. They appear together within the framework of teacher influence.

109

Sources of influence. In their scholarly discussion of social power and influence as a relationship between two agents, French and Raven structure their theory on the basis of the perceptions of the recipients of the influence.[5] Especially important to these investigators were five possible sources or bases of power within the influencing agent: (1) reward power, based on one's perception that the other has the power to mediate rewards for him; (2) coercive power, based on one's perception that the other has the ability to mediate punishments for him; (3) legitimate power, based on one's perception that the other has a legitimate right to prescribe behavior for him; (4) referent power, based on one's willingness and capacity to identify with the other; and (5) expert power, based on one's perception that the other has some special knowledge or expertise.

Certainly, every type of power base as here defined is part of any instructor's potential weaponry in establishing a viable relationship with his pupils. Here, however, reward power and coercive power were lessened considerably and hopefully eliminated by Mr. T's continuous reminders that the pupils would not be graded, tested, or otherwise singled out for reward or punishment based on their outside reading or lack of it. Of course, this does not mean that all pupils took him at his word, and some part of their effort may indeed have been directed to this end. In view of the teacher's statements, however, it is unlikely that the pursuit of better grades would be the main spur for the pupils' reading activity. Only one pupil, G15, who was the heaviest user, even mentioned grades during the interview in response to question 3a, and since it was not her major consideration, the response was not recorded. We do treat the subject of grades, however, later when dealing with pupil motivation.

Most important here are the bases of referent power and expert power which are directly related to the premise we have advanced. It is in this respect that we present our rationale for the use of media as a voluntary activity for which French and Raven have provided the framework. Concerning referent power, if the pupil is highly attracted to his teacher he will desire a close association with him, corresponding to Cogan's symbolic proximity, as described in chapter 3. The pupil perceives that this identification or proximity can be established and maintained if he behaves and believes as does his teacher. Concerning expert power, the strength of this source of influence varies with the degree or level of expertise ascribed to the teacher by the pupil. He probably evaluates his teacher's expertise in relation to his own, as well as against an absolute standard.

Legitimate power also enters the picture since it is clearly an internalized value within pupils that a teacher has a legitimate right to influence them. This initial obligation on the part of the pupil to accept a teacher's influence is a necessary characteristic of any situation in which learning is expected to take place. Without it, say in the case of teachers operating with groups of different cultural and social values, conflicts are sure to develop unless certain special measures are taken to overcome these barriers. With our sample, of course, legitimate power presents itself and interrelates with the other bases of influence. Obviously, the degree to which a pupil feels the obligation is determined by his receptiveness to the teacher as a referent or desirable acquaintance and his recognition of the teacher as an expert. Thus we have an adequate explanation for the potential influence of our Mr. T.

GUIDANCE AS A FACTOR

We have recognized guidance as a teacher characteristic to be treated as part of teacher influence. This need not have been the case had it been possible to utilize the services of a third person, a neutral party such as the media specialist, to promote the use of materials with another class taught by Mr. T. Effects of this activity could have been measured in terms of library use and compared to the effects of the teacher on the experimental group. This was not possible, however, and the teacher provided all guidance used in this study. We need not apologize for this, however, since the direction of bibliographic effort is, in our opinion, the teacher's responsibility.

This responsibility when taken seriously reflects the position of bibliographic guidance as one more factor used to establish the type of attitude within the pupil which would make him receptive to the teacher's suggestions. Bibliographic guidance certainly should enhance the pupils' idea of the teacher as an expert in his field; and, if undertaken in a way that would indicate a personal interest in the welfare of the pupils, it should also enhance the teacher's image as a desirable personality. Therefore, we include it within the scope of teacher influence.

SUBJECT INTEREST AS A FACTOR

Although this is a pupil characteristic rather than one of the teacher, it has been shown in previous research not to be entirely independent of the effects of teacher influence. Many pupils have come to favor certain subjects over others, not necessarily because they had more proficiency in the former, but rather because they had better teachers. Of course, there are other elements at work including that of natural ability in the field which combine to shape the pupils' opinion regarding a curricular offering. Pupils' feelings for a subject would necessarily be relevant to any study which seeks to determine why the pupils were moved to perform extra effort in it.

111

Therefore, the rating scale, in addition to eliciting the pupils' opinions of the teacher, also concerns their general attitude toward the field of mathematics as an academic endeavor. It was, therefore, given separate treatment. We fully expected that the attitude toward the subject would approximate rather closely their opinion of the teacher; but we also felt strongly that interest in mathematics alone could not account for anything more than infrequent use of mathematics materials.

SATISFACTION WITH MEDIA AS A FACTOR

The fourth possible cause is the pupils' satisfaction with the media they had used. The satisfaction of a need or interest is readily seen as a probable cause for repeated use of the materials in the bibliography. Circumstances surrounding the first use, however, cannot be explained in these terms. Teacher influence again would appear to be operating in respect to the first felt need of the pupil to use the materials.

Of course, satisfaction with materials is a legitimate consideration in an analysis of the reasons behind student use. Lack of satisfaction may well serve to explain pupils' failure to use media center materials more than once. Likewise, it is easy to see that a frustration factor may be operating here in the possible failure to find desired materials at the time they are needed. This conceivably could result in a negative attitude toward the media center which affects the future use of its resources. Information gleaned in the interview does much to clarify some of these points.

The Case for Teacher Influence

INTERVIEW RESULTS—EXPERIMENTAL GROUP

In response to question 1, fifteen pupils felt that the teacher wanted them to acquire new information and better understanding, while two pupils felt that interest and enjoyment on their part was the teacher's purpose. It is interesting to note that the two pupils who stressed the recreational aspect borrowed only one mathematics item between them. This may be an attempt to justify their lack of response to his urgings or, on the other hand, may really account for it. Question 2 reveals that 15 pupils thought the teacher was right in mentioning books, eight of them indicating that it was his responsibility to do so, while seven pupils stated that additional information is acquired through reading. One pupil, G16, was undecided and only one pupil, G23, felt the instructor was wrong because it took up too much time.

Question 3 related directly to the reasons for the use or lack of use of materials, and we see that of the 10 pupils who used the library more than once, seven felt that it was the teacher's emphasis which made them feel the materials were important and they sought to show him that they were interested. Of the five top-ranked pupils in terms of circulation, only G23 was missing from this group. Here we have the clearest indication of the effect of teacher influence and the feeling is shared by the heaviest users. The other three pupils mentioned personal characteristics such as information and interest needs.

Of the five pupils who used the library only once, four claimed lack of time as a reason. This claim appears to have been justified, and responses to question 5 show that of this group only pupil G3 (who borrowed three items on that one occasion of use) was disappointed with the materials. Since she had waited until the seventh week to use the library, however, it is doubtful that her disappointment caused her relative lack of use. One pupil, B16 (who had emphasized the recreational purpose in his response to question 1) did not want to spend too much time on nonrequired work. The two pupils who did not use library materials were of similar mind in declaring their rather casual approach to optional efforts.

Question 4 examines the factor of satisfaction with materials directly and provides information necessary to rank the pupils in this regard. Six pupils declared themselves to be completely satisfied with the helpful and interesting nature of the materials. Included in the group is pupil G15, the heaviest user, but also included are pupils G16, G17, and B14 who used materials only once due to a lack of time.

Not entirely satisfied were seven pupils, six of whom used mathematics materials on at least two occasions but found some materials much less interesting than others. The remaining pupil (B16 again) used materials only once, a filmstrip which he found less interesting and more difficult than he expected. Two pupils expressed disappointment, including the aforementioned G3 who used library materials only during the seventh week, as well as G23 who consistently used the library three weeks in succession and accounted for eight circulations.

The responses to question 5 indicate that eight pupils were always able to get what they wanted from the library, while seven pupils were not. In the former group were two pupils who used the library only once each due to lack of time. The latter group included three pupils who used the library only once (G3, B14, and B16). Thus the frustration factor could not account for the failure to use the library more than once in more than three cases.

Question 7 reveals that 13 pupils found materials in mathematics to be somewhat enjoyable and four of them also felt that their grade benefitted. Among this group of four was the heaviest user, pupil G15, as well as pupil G17 who used the materials only once. The general consensus among users, whether frequent or infrequent, was that materials in mathematics provided enjoyment but very little help in achieving their grade.

INTERVIEW RESULTS—CONTROL GROUP

The nonlibrary aspect of mathematics is seen in response to question 5 which shows that 16 of the 17 pupils do not think about mathematics when in the library. Only two of these pupils, however, in response to question 6-b felt that mathematics materials are not enjoyable. Sixteen pupils also believed that mathematics materials could be helpful in clarifying concepts, while only one individual felt that such materials would not relate to work done in class. We were encouraged in our appreciation for the teacher's role in that there appeared to be a willingness on the part of pupils in this group to use such items, but in the absence of any bibliographic direction on the part of the teacher, they did not think about it.

The special questions from the experimental group interview schedule given to pupil G12, the only user in the control group, produced similar responses to those given by members of the experimental group. In other words, here is a pupil with a basic interest in the study of mathematics, who was satisfied with the material and who was always successful in getting what she wanted from the media center. The fact remains, however, that without the teacher's bibliographic activity she was inclined to borrow only one mathematics book from the media center during the first fifteen weeks of school.

SUMMARY OF INTERVIEW RESPONSES

In our interviews we had given primary consideration to the assessment of the factor of pupils' satisfaction with materials, question 4 of the experimental group interview schedule providing data in this regard. We found the case for pupils' satisfaction with materials as the causal element to be damaged considerably. Following is a review of the facts regarding the experimental group:

1. Of the six pupils who declared themselves to be fully satisfied with the materials, three of them were one-time users.
2. Six of the seven pupils who were not entirely satisfied with materials used them on at least two occasions.
3. One of the two pupils who was dissatisfied with the materials used them three weeks in succession and accounted for eight loans.
4. Of the five pupils who used the media center only once, only one was dissatisfied while three were completely satisfied.

5. The general consensus was that the materials were enjoyable but not very helpful in achieving grades.

The control group data indicated a similar lack of support for the satisfaction factor:

1. Pupil G12 was fully satisfied and had high interest in mathematics but charged out only one item.
2. The consensus was that library materials in mathematics were interesting and possibly helpful but pupils did not think about mathematics when in the library.

Support for the teacher influence factor. The results of the interviews, while eroding the credibility of pupils' satisfaction with materials as a cause, reveal data in support of the premise of the investigation, that of teacher influence. These are:

1. Of the 10 pupils who used the library for mathematics on more than one occasion, seven stated that the reason they did so was the teacher's emphasis on them and their desire to show him that they were interested.
2. Three users of the film loop indicated that the teacher's special emphasis on it led them to use it.
3. Three pupils in the control group knew of the use of media center materials by the other class, but did not feel inclined to use them because their teacher did not say anything about it to them.

Of course, such findings by themselves are rather inconclusive but further evidence to support our position follows.

RATING SCALE RESULTS

The rating scale was designed solely to help explain the causal relationship, and produced data which was subjected to statistical analysis. It provided a measure of the esteem in which the teacher was held by members of the experimental group and, in doing so, produced a means of predicting the degree of his influence in getting them to do nonrequired reading. By being personable and efficient, the teacher possesses the necessary qualities of an influential instructor. The other factor considered as a possible causal element for which data are provided by the rating scale is that of subject interest.

As in the case of teacher influence, it was possible to compare this factor to the circulation record of each pupil to determine whether or not

115

a relationship exists. We predicted that the quality of teacher influence as represented by the scores given in the student rating of the teacher would correlate with the circulation rate for each pupil, although this would not necessarily be true of subject interest and circulation rate. We did expect to find a relationship, however, between teacher influence and subject interest, since we have pointed out that such interest depends to a great extent on the effectiveness of the teacher.

Mr. T, an influential teacher. An examination of tables 16 and 17 reveals the high degree of agreement between the two groups of pupils in their feelings for the teacher and the subject. Mr. T in each case received a mean score of 4.88 based on a five point scale. This was a composite score of personality and ability and served in each case to rank him second of 12 teachers named. We fully expected then, that having this kind of power base, Mr. T would be an influential teacher. By the same reasoning, it would be expected that teachers H and K, on the low end of the scale with both groups, would not be influential types and would have trouble getting pupils to perform optional tasks. Had time and resources permitted, this would have made an interesting and valuable point to be pursued.

High interest in mathematics. The ratings of the groups on their interest in mathematics also closely approximated each other with a mean score of 4.06 for the experimental group and 4.00 for the control group. In the case of the former, this was good enough for first rank among major subjects whereas in the case of the latter group it produced only a tie with foreign language for second rank. Despite the difference in ranks, the interest in mathematics is approximately the same. One cannot say that a real difference exists between the two groups in their willingness to use mathematics materials based on this factor. To support this statement the following pages provide a summary of correlational analyses of the factors of teacher influence, subject interest, and pupils' satisfaction with materials (the last factor based on data provided by interview question 4) with respect to the circulation rate of the experimental group. Teacher influence and subject interest are also compared since we felt that a relationship exists between the two.

USE OF KENDALL'S TAU

A detailed explanation of this statistic is provided by Siegel,[6] but briefly it is a method employed in arriving at a correlation coefficient when data for two variables are at least of ordinal nature. It is employed as an alternative to Spearman's rho and is considered by Blalock to be more useful and more satisfactory whenever the number of ties is quite large.[7] It was used here to provide a measure of the association between the circulation

TABLE 16. EXPERIMENTAL GROUP RATING SCALE RESULTS

(a) INDIVIDUAL RATINGS OF MR. T AND INTEREST IN MATHEMATICS

PUPIL	ABILITY	RATING OF TEACHER PERSONALITY	COMPOSITE	INTEREST IN MATHEMATICS
B1	5	5	5	4
G3	5	5	5	5
B8	5	5	5	3
G11	4	5	4.5	2
G14	5	5	5	5
G15	5	5	5	4
B14	5	5	5	5
G16	5	4	4.5	1
G17	5	4	4.5	5
B16	5	5	5	5
G19	5	5	5	4
G20	5	5	5	5
B23	5	5	5	4
G22	5	5	5	5
B21	5	5	5	5
G23	5	5	5	4
G24	5	4	4.5	4
Mean	4.94	4.82	4.88	4.06

(b) RANKING OF TEACHERS BY COMPOSITE RATING

RANK	TEACHER	SCORE	RESPONSES
1	A	4.95	9
2	Mr. T	4.88	17
3	B	4.84	15
4	C	4.70	5
5	D	4.50	14
5	E	4.50	1
7	F	4.33	3
8	G	4.25	2
9	H	4.00	1
9	I	4.00	1
11	J	3.50	1
12	K	2.50	1

(c) RANKING OF SUBJECTS BY INTEREST SCORES

RANK	SUBJECT	SCORE	RESPONSES
1	Mathematics	4.06	17
2	Science	4.00	4
3	English	3.71	17
4	Language	3.67	15
5	Soc. Studies	3.65	17

TABLE 17. CONTROL GROUP RATING SCALE RESULTS

(a) INDIVIDUAL RATINGS OF MR. T AND INTEREST IN MATHEMATICS

| PUPIL | RATING OF TEACHER | | | INTEREST IN |
	ABILITY	PERSONALITY	COMPOSITE	MATHEMATICS
G2	5	5	5	5
G5	4	5	4.5	2
G6	4	5	4.5	4
B4	5	5	5	5
B5	5	5	5	4
G8	5	5	5	5
B6	4	5	4.5	5
G9	5	5	5	4
B10	5	5	5	4
B11	5	5	5	5
G10	5	5	5	3
G12	5	5	5	5
B15	5	5	4.5	4
B17	5	5	5	5
B24	5	4	4.5	1
G26	5	5	5	4
G27	5	5	5	3
Mean	4.82	4.94	4.88	4.00

(b) RANKING OF TEACHERS BY COMPOSITE RATING

RANK	TEACHER	SCORE	RESPONSES
1	N	5.00	1
2	Mr. T	4.88	17
3	F	4.75	12
3	B	4.75	8
3	D	4.75	6
6	I	4.72	7
7	C	4.58	7
8	L	4.00	1
8	O	4.00	1
10	H	3.75	2
10	K	3.75	2
12	G	3.63	8

(c) RANKING OF SUBJECTS BY INTEREST SCORES

RANK	SUBJECT	SCORE	RESPONSES
1	Science	4.11	13
2	Mathematics	4.00	17
2	Language	4.00	8
4	English	3.53	17
5	Soc. Studies	2.77	17

rate and each of the three variables regarded as possible causal elements. Although one cannot infer a cause-effect relationship from positive correlation, without it a viable theory is impossible.

The mechanics of the statistical application are explained rather fully in Appendix H and need not be a matter of concern here. Let it suffice to say that in these correlational analyses, the null hypothesis, H_0, states that there is no association between the two variables for which chance alone cannot account. The level of significance needed for rejection of this premise is again 0.05. For full description of the computation of the tau statistic for each of the associations, the reader should refer to the original study;[8] but for our purposes it is enough to summarize briefly the results.

Teacher influence the only tenable explanation. In applying the statistical test, we find that of the three possible causes only our favored teacher influence (pupil esteem or rating of the teacher) is significant in its association with mathematics media circulation. The probability, here, is 0.055, only slightly above the critical value of 0.05. What this means is that in 5.5 cases of 100, rather than the required 5 cases, would a correlation of this nature be attributable to chance. The difference is slight and adds support to our belief inasmuch as the other two possibilities are demolished in a convincing fashion.

Interest in mathematics when related to circulation rate produced a probability of only 0.480. This simply means that chance alone could account for the demonstrated association 48 percent of the time. Obviously there is no correlation whatsoever.

Even more removed was the factor of pupils' satisfaction with materials in its relationship to mathematics circulation. Oddly enough, here we had a negative correlation, or the unusual condition of satisfied pupils using fewer mathematics titles than unsatisfied or dissatisfied individuals. The probability of $-.201$ indicates that there is a 20 percent possibility that this result was due to chance alone, which is quite conceivable in these circumstances; that is, unless one chooses to believe that less satisfied pupils used more mathematics items in an effort to find something that satisfied them (not beyond the realm of reason).

In using such statistical devices one must remember that the final answer has not been rendered. The fact is that the sample was small and did not offer opportunity to discriminate as one might have wished. On the other hand, we now have evidence to support our belief regarding the value of an influential teacher in stimulating media center use, since the factor of teacher influence reigned supreme over the acknowledged alternatives. When coupled with the supportive statements gleaned from the interviews, we have a solid basis for our contention.

119

Teacher influence and interest in mathematics. The last correlation performed was with respect to the relationship between an influential teacher and pupil interest in his subject, since we did feel positive about this. The results substantiated our beliefs, since the demonstrated probability of 0.063 was second only to the relationship between teacher influence and mathematics media circulation. Although not at the 0.05 level, there is reason to think that by virtue of his or her influence, a good teacher makes a class interesting.

MOTIVATION OF PUPILS

All along we have felt that our position has been a logical one inasmuch as we regard the responsiveness of pupils to the suggestions of their teacher as a measure of his or her influence. That the esteem in which the teacher is held by his or her pupils is the chief determinant of the degree to which he or she holds such power is posited in the study. In the remaining pages of this chapter we examine the types of ploys used by the teacher to influence the reading of his charges. Next we study the effect of grades and then conclude with a treatment of the changed behavior of pupils.

Activities of an influential teacher. If Mr. T is truly an influential teacher, effects of that influence must be evident in respect to the strength of the pupils' reading activity. The strongest weapon in the possession of any teacher obviously lies within the framework of his or her use of coercive or reward power, the grades themselves. That is not the case in this study, however, when the task is not a required one and rather takes the form of a suggested activity. In keeping with our premise, we felt that the strongest appeal possible was one which would affect the pupil's relationship to the teacher, either as a beneficiary of his expertise or even more importantly as a recipient of his good will and favor.

With this in mind, we categorized three different ploys in terms of the degree to which the teacher was personally involved in each. When media were mentioned by the teacher on any day during the test period other than Monday (when introductions of all materials were given), these bibliographic activities or reinforcements were classified according to the teacher's tone representing the degree of involvement or importance ascribed by him to the effort. These were (1) general ploys, (2) hopeful ploys, or (3) disappointment ploys.

Least personal involvement was present or least care was shown in the general ploy in which Mr. T described the qualities of certain titles or the books in general. Next was the hopeful ploy when he stated and possibly reiterated his desire that the media should be used. The strongest ploy in terms of personal involvement was that of disappointment in which Mr. T felt "discouraged" by reports from the "librarian" that the pupils were not using the materials very much. The gist of this appeal was that although he had not checked up on them and would not do so in the future, he was rather unhappy that the pupils were not more appreciative of the hours of work he had spent in the selection of titles.

Results—further support for the concept of influence. Table 18 gives the rate of circulation as well as the percentage figures for days in which introductions and reinforcements occurred as compared to those days in which media were not mentioned by the teacher. We can see that titles circulated on 18 of the 24 days in which bibliographic activity occurred for a proportion of 75 percent. On the other hand, materials circulated on only three of the fourteen days in which no titles were mentioned, a proportion of 21 percent. The picture thus is clearly drawn with respect to responsiveness of pupils to the activity of the teacher.

It becomes even clearer when one analyzes the circulation totals. Bibliographic-activity days accounted for 82 mathematics loans or 91 percent of the total mathematics circulation figure while consuming only 63 percent of the total number of days in the test period. In contrast, days without bibliographic activity comprise 37 percent of the total number of days but account for only 9 percent of the circulation. The best indicator of a "happening" is the circulation rate figure. There is a striking contrast between the 3.4 mathematics items circulated for each day in which bibliographic activity occurs and the rate of 0.6 items for each day without such activity.

Table 19 presents a good overview of pupil responsiveness. The disappointment ploy was used only twice and, as we expected, did account for a high incidence of pupil use (18 loans, or a rate of 9.0 per activity). The hopeful ploy was next in producing 23 loans on the seven days it was used, or 3.3 per activity. Last came the general ploy which represented a total of 16 charges for its seven occasions of use, or 2.3 per activity. These results were exactly as predicted within the framework of our hypothesis and clearly reflect the presence of teacher influence as interpreted in the study. The more personally involved the teacher was with his appeal, the higher the rate of response by the pupils.

How much time needed? The significant point concerning the time element is how little of it was necessary. Mr. T participated in bibliographic activity 24 days of the test period for an average of four minutes per activity. It is interesting to note that for the entire period of eight weeks, he spent only 96 minutes of class time in such efforts. Of course, this would not reflect the number of work hours spent in the selection of items or preparation of the bibliographies which amounted to about 24 hours or three hours per week for the six-item listings. It does answer quite well, however, the criticism lodged against this type of work by many mathe-

TABLE 18. Rate and Percentage of Mathematics Media Use on Days with and without Teacher's Bibliographic Activity

	CIRCULATION DAYS	%	NON-CIRC. DAYS
Days with bibliographic activity	18	47%	6
Days without bibliographic activity	3	8%	11
Total	21	55%	17

matics teachers, that they cannot afford the time in class. Also, with respect to the time involved in preparation of bibliographies, too many teachers are unaware of the resources and services offered to them by the school media center and too few media specialists take initiative in publicizing the bibliographic function or their willingness to undertake it. This is especially true in the case of mathematics. Be that as it may, those 96 minutes of class time spent in bibliographic awareness did produce a definite change in the reading habits of the youngsters.

Effect of grades. It is difficult to assess the role of grades in the pupils' inclination to use mathematics materials in this study. Since Mr. T made continued efforts to reassure the pupils that they were not being checked and that neither reward nor punishment would follow with respect to their reading activity, it was expected that the influence of this element was

TABLE 19. Type and Duration of Teacher's Bibliographic Activity and Resulting Circulation Rate

	INTRODUCTIONS	REINFORCEMENTS			TOTAL	TOTAL
		G	H	D	R	I & R
No. of activities	8	7	7	2	16	24
Minutes duration	56	14	13	13	40	96
Minutes/activity	7.0	2.0	1.9	6.5	2.5	4.0
No. of circ. days	6	4	6	2	12	18
No. of Circulations	25	16	23	18	57	82
Circ. rate/activity	3.1	2.3	3.3	9.0	3.6	3.4

G = general ploy   H = hopeful ploy   D = disappointed ploy
I = introductions   R = reinforcements

122

%	TOTALS	%	NO. OF CIRC.	%	DAILY CIRC. RATE
16%	24	63%	82	91%	3.4
29%	14	37%	8	9%	.6
45%	38	100%	90	100%	

minor. Only the heaviest user, pupil G15, even alluded to the grade in discussing her reasons for using the materials; she also pointed out that this was not her major consideration.

Table 20 compares the mathematics circulation rate both prior to and subsequent to the issue of grades during the fourth week of the test period. A dramatic rise in the number of loans occurred during the fourth week, but we cannot ascribe the increased level of use and its subsequent maintenance as being a function of grades. Obviously, the grades bore little capacity to discriminate since 15 of the 17 pupils received the highest achievement score of five while the other two received the next highest grade of four.

The circulation rate doubled during the five weeks subsequent to grades as compared to the three weeks which preceded them, as 11 pupils increased their circulation rate while only four pupils showed a decrease. Two pupils maintained the same level of reading activity, no mathematics items at all. Of the 11 pupils whose use of mathematics materials had heightened, one received a grade of four. The other recipient of a four was never moved to use a title, and the four pupils who used fewer mathematics items all received a grade of five.

Two pupils used mathematics materials before but not after grades were given, while seven pupils used materials only after the grading period. Six pupils used materials both before and after grades were received. In all, there were eight users prior to the fourth week and thirteen users (six of them repeats) subsequent to the grading period. Not much can be said of the effects of grades on the disposition to use the library. From the evidence gathered, the effect appears to be slight. We prefer to believe that the increasing influence of the teacher due to his continuous bibliographic activity was chiefly responsible for the increased rate of circulation subsequent to the grading period.

123

TABLE 20. First Quarter Grades and Mathematics Circulation Rate for Members of the Experimental Group

PUPILS	GRADES (1–5 SCALE)	WEEKLY CIRC. RATE PRIOR TO GRADES	WEEKLY CIRC. RATE AFTER GRADES	AMOUNT OF CHANGE
B1	5	0	.6	+ .6
G3	5	0	.6	+ .6
B8	5	1.0	.4	− .6
G11	4	0	0	0
G14	5	1.0	.6	− .4
G15	5	3.3	3.6	+ .3
B14	5	.3	0	− .3
G16	5	.3	0	− .3
G17	5	0	.2	+ .2
B16	4	0	.2	+ .2
G19	5	.3	.8	+ .5
G20	5	.6	1.2	+ .6
B23	5	.3	.4	+ .1
G22	5	0	2.6	+2.6
B21	5	0	0	0
G23	5	0	1.6	+1.6
G24	5	0	1.0	+1.0

Mean = .4   Mean = .8

Changes in Reading Behavior

Now let us pause and reflect on the results. Basically we have caused a dramatic change in the reading behavior of a group of junior high school students by recognizing the important position of the teacher. When Mr. T took an active interest in imparting bibliographic awareness and encouragement to use library media related to the topics being taught in class, the pupils responded by using these titles. The increased reading activity occurred despite the fact that the media center was relatively inaccessible to the majority of the pupils, since they had no free periods. It occurred despite the fact that the subject was mathematics, categorized as a minor user of the library in previous research and generally overlooked by pupils when library materials are selected. Possibly most important, it occurred despite the fact that the nature of the task was optional rather than required and did not count for extra credit. Thus we are able to identify the motivation device as the influential teacher.

124

Somewhat discouraging is the fact that immediately upon withdrawal of Mr. T's bibliographic activity, the members of the experimental group ceased to use mathematics media and reverted to the same behavior they demonstrated previously. French and Raven discuss in scholarly fashion the phenomenon of dependence on an external agent, and relating their theory to the present study makes it easier to understand.[9] Essentially, the teacher has served as a change agent or catalyst for the altered bibliographic activity of the test period and his active involvement maintained the new condition throughout its brief history. That the change in pupils' reading behavior was completely dependent on the teacher involvement was proven once this activity ceased, for the reading pattern of the experimental group then reverted to its original state.

The question naturally follows as to whether it is possible for the teacher to influence the internalization of such values within his pupils so that they will continue as readers of mathematics materials, even if he does not continue to promote the value of such media and encourage their use. Clearly, this question cannot be answered here since it would require analysis of pupils' characteristics as well as teacher influence. This internalization has probably occurred to some degree as a result of conditioning (which includes teachers' activities) in those subjects regarded as major users of the media center, such as social studies and English. Although it may be possible in the case of mathematics, it is doubtful that such internalized effects can be realized over a short period of time such as that covered in our study.

Notes

1. Hubert M. Blalock, *Social Statistics* (2d ed.; New York: McGraw-Hill, 1972), p. 285.

2. Ibid., p. 295.

3. Ronald D. Blazek, "Teacher Utilization of Nonrequired Library Materials in Mathematics and the Effect on Pupil Use" (Unpublished Ph.D. dissertation, Univ. of Illinois, 1971), pp. 146–61.

4. Blalock, *Social Statistics*, pp. 233–35.

5. John R. P. French and Bertrand Raven, "The Bases of Social Power," in Dorwin Cartwright and Alvin Zander, eds., *Group Dynamics Research and Theory*, (3d ed.; New York: Harper, 1968), pp. 263–68.

6. Sidney Siegel, *Nonparametric Statistics for the Behavioral Sciences* (New York: McGraw-Hill, 1956), pp. 213–23.

7. Blalock, *Social Statistics*, p. 421.

8. Blazek, "Teacher Utilization," pp. 207–14.

9. French and Raven, "The Bases of Social Power," pp. 261–62.

5

Understanding the Professional Responsibilities

What We Did

The purpose of our study was to examine the change in pupil use patterns when a teacher utilized media center resources as part of his teaching routine. The nature of the task was optional rather than required and focused attention on the supplementary materials in the field of mathematics. The discipline of mathematics was chosen because in the past there has been a lack of communication between media specialists and mathematics teachers which has resulted in a general neglect of mathematics resources by pupils. The focal points for the study were the teacher's library role and the manner in which pupils could be influenced to use the media center without threat of punishment or promise of reward. From this we gained insight into the media specialist's responsibility to the educational enterprise.

It was incumbent that we consider the areas of teacher competence, teacher behavior, and teacher effectiveness, the results of which reflect our choice of teacher influence as the causal element. We have interpreted this factor broadly and represent it as a statement of dual nature involving the pupil's respect for the teacher as a subject matter authority and/or their identification with him as a desirable personality. In addition to teacher influence, the factors of guidance, subject interest, and pupils' satisfaction with materials were recognized as possible causes. All except guidance were measured separately and analyzed.

What constitutes a difference in this study from those in the past dealing with the teacher's role was our choice of the experimental method in its design. Past studies have been largely of a descriptive nature and depended to a great extent on the teacher's assessment of his own qualities and attitudes regarding the library. These have been obtained traditionally through questionnaires or interviews. The problem here, we feel, is that the

126

teacher's recorded sentiments do not necessarily register his or her actual involvement, since it is one thing to recognize the value of the media center but quite another to do something about it. The advantage in our experimental method is that we were able to control completely the teacher's use of materials. Thus, we were able to analyze in direct manner the effects of this variable on student use.

One teacher was chosen with two classes of subfreshman level at University High School, the laboratory school of the University of Illinois. The teacher passed out bibliographies to members of the experimental group each Monday during the eight week test period. These bibliographies consisted of four book titles (two skill mastery or concept development type, one history-background type, and one recreational type), one film-strip or film loop, and one periodical article. The number of reinforcements or occasions in which the teacher mentioned the media subsequent to the Monday introduction was varied each week as was also the degree of his personal involvement in them. In this way, we could analyze the changes in student use patterns. Circulation records were kept not only for the two groups, but also for a third class of subfreshman mathematics taught by another teacher. Since this group was composed of pupils with lower arithmetic achievement scores, it did not serve as part of the control but did afford the opportunity for additional comparisons in library use.

Prior to the test period, we engaged in a pretest of six weeks during which the use of the media center by the different groups was recorded. This was done so that we could determine the disposition of the pupils to use media prior to the teacher's bibliographic activity. We judged the experimental group to be homogenous with the control group in aptitudes and abilities, although we did find that the control group had a greater degree of accessibility to the media center owing to a greater number of free periods. Thus, if the results of the experiment were positive, the experimental group using more materials in significant fashion, it would represent the overcoming of the obstacle of relative inaccessibility.

Also, there was a post-test of six weeks in which the media center activity of the groups was again recorded and the teacher ceased all mention of materials in either class. We did this in order to determine the amount of carryover or general effect of the teacher with members of the experimental group from the preceding period. Also, we took the opportunity to note the effect on members of the control group of the information provided them by the investigator, of the existence and availability of mathematics items. If the teacher influence factor were, indeed, of predominant importance, we would expect that the knowledge provided by the neutral party would have little effect on the pupils' inclination to use library materials.

127

We tested the following hypothesis: The *greater the teacher utilization of media center resources in his teaching, the greater the use of the center by pupils because in their recognition of the teacher as a subject matter authority they will emulate his manner of acquiring knowledge and/or in their regard for him as a desirable personality will seek to please him.* In addition, the mathematics materials borrowed by members of the experimental group were compared on the basis of form and content. From the rating scale and interview of pupils we received added insight both into the nature of causality and into the pupils preferences for certain forms or types of supplementary materials.

What We Found

CIRCULATION OF MATERIALS

As we expected, results of the pretest showed no real differences between groups in either number of users or circulation figures. Both the control group and Miss M's group borrowed more materials than did the experimental group but not to a significant degree. Of vital importance is the fact that there were absolutely no mathematics items charged to anybody at this time. This mirrors the general neglect of such materials in the school media center, the condition which we had chosen to alter.

That we were successful was best seen by the dramatic change in the reading activity of the experimental group during the test period. All 17 pupils charged at least one item from the media center and only two of them failed to use a mathematics title. There were 91 loans of mathematics materials and 66 loans of other materials for a circulation total of 157. This more than doubled the total of 76 charges by the control group membership and 59 by members of Miss M's group. There was only one mathematics title borrowed in the control group and none in Miss M's group. Our application of statistical tests indicated that the differences between the experimental and control groups in circulation and in number of users were significant not only with respect to mathematics materials but extended as well to total use of all materials including mathematics. The change, although of great proportions, proved to be only temporary in nature.

Once the test period had ended and the teacher had ceased his bibliographic activity, there was a return by the experimental group to the reading pattern exhibited during the pretest. During the post-test, there was as great a decrease in the use of mathematics materials as there was an increase during the preceding period, and the relative ranks of the three groups in total circulation returned to that of the pretest. The experimental group again was last of the three, although the differences again were not significant. The experimental and control groups each borrowed one item in mathematics, the one in the experimental group resulting from an inadvertent mention of the title by the teacher. Miss M's group continued to ignore mathematics materials.

In analyzing the media center performance of the experimental group over the three periods, results show a significant increase from the pretest to the test period and a significant decrease from the test period to the post-test. This is true of mathematics media when considered separately and of total media center use, including mathematics materials. We were able to see that the use of mathematics materials was high enough during the test 'period to establish the experimental group's superiority in total use as well. Thus, we have a clear indication of the effects of the independent variable, teacher utilization, in the resulting reading behavior patterns of pupils.

Briefly, we established that the experimental group belonged to a different population of media center users during the test period when teacher utilization was present than it did during the pretest and post-test when teacher utilization was absent. Of special interest is the fact that the population of media center users was the same during the pretest prior to the teacher's activity as it was during the post-test after the teacher had terminated his involvement. During these two periods, both the experimental and control groups were almost exactly alike.

Conclusions. Concerning the circulation of media center materials are three important points:

1. The hypothesis of the study which predicts a relationship between the utilization of nonrequired media center-based materials by the math teacher in his teaching routine and the use of these media by the students is supported by the data.
2. There is a general neglect by students of media center resources in mathematics. This pattern can be changed, however, through the efforts of a teacher.
3. Relative inaccessibility to the media center does not serve as a deterrent to its use by students who are motivated by an influential teacher.

FORMS OF MEDIA

Another consideration was the types of mathematics materials borrowed by members of the experimental group. Film material and recreational books showed the highest mean weekly circulation rate per title for the test period, averaging 3.0 and 2.9 loans respectively. This was more than double the mean weekly rate per title of the other three types of materials: concept development or skill mastery books (1.4), history-background books (1.4), and periodical articles (1.3).

It is most interesting to note that the film material was of concept development type if analyzed by content. The similarity of use of these items to that of recreational books appears to be an indication of the manner in which pupils tend to view such materials. If the projected image is considered to be enjoyable or less taxing mentally, this would explain the preference for film when pupils are given a choice. In treating all types of books together as a form, the book averaged 1.9 loans per title per week. This was higher than the periodical but lower than the film.

Seven of the ten users of film material in the experimental group did indeed indicate at the time of the interview that they felt film to be easier or more interesting than books, which supports our contention. Nine members of the experimental group thought books were of primary importance in mathematics but that film should also be used. Eight others felt that the two media were of equal importance. Responses of 13 members of the group indicated that they felt film to be of equal value in the study of history, while four pupils stated that books were of primary importance but both media should be used. Film was not considered important to the study of English. Control group responses were similar, although there were slight differences. A vital point was the consensus among members of both groups that library media in mathematics were interesting and enjoyable. Here is our definite indicator that there exists a potential, largely unrealized, for the use of supplementary media of various kinds in the teaching of mathematics.

Conclusions. Thus we are able to arrive at two conclusions which should prove valuable in planning for the education of the young:

1. Supplementary materials in mathematics are many and varied, and students consider such materials to be interesting and enjoyable.
2. Film material is identified by students as being enjoyable and less taxing mentally than books. Both books and film are considered by them to be important in the study of mathematics and of history. There is little regard for the use of film in English.

REASONS FOR STUDENT USE

Our final concern was with causality. We employed three possible causes in tests of association with pupils' use of mathematics items. The rating scale provided the necessary information regarding both teacher influence and subject interest. The interview provided us with a measure of the pupils' satisfaction with materials. Bibliographic guidance was not examined separately and we considered it to be within the framework of teacher influence. Our fourth correlation tested the relationship between teacher influence and subject interest where we had predicted an association to exist.

Happily, the results of these analyses generally followed the pattern predicted by the study. Neither subject interest nor pupils' satisfaction with materials approached a significant level in terms of their relationship to pupils' use; in fact, the satisfaction factor produced a negative correlation. Only the composite rating of the teacher's personality and expertise (teacher influence) produced a relationship which was just about statistically significant. Failure to establish this definitely we felt was due primarily to the small sample size and the inability to distinguish differences among the members of the group in their feelings for the teacher, since they all thought highly of him. The same was true of the correlation between teacher influence and subject interest.

The results of the personal interview provided us with further support in our belief that teacher influence must be of primary importance:

1. Of the ten pupils who used the media center for mathematics on more than one occasion, seven stated that the reason was the teacher's emphasis on the materials and that it was their desire to show him that they were interested.
2. Three users of the film loop indicated that the teacher's special emphasis on it led them to use it.
3. Three pupils in the control group knew of the use of materials by the other class but did not feel inclined to use them because their teacher did not say anything to them.

Finally, we identified three types of ploys or appeals made by the teacher in his bibliographic activity and found added support favoring teacher influence as the causal element. As it turned out, the more personally involved the teacher was with the appeal he made, the more responsive were the pupils. The appeal which represented the highest degree of personal involvement was his disappointment regarding "reports from the media specialist" that the materials were not being used.

The disappointment ploy was used twice and produced an extraordinary response of 18 charges or 9.0 per activity. The next appeal in terms of personal involvement was one in which the teacher was hopeful that the materials would be used. The hopeful ploy was used seven times and resulted in 23 loans for a rate of 3.3 per activity. The appeal of general nature, in which the teacher simply described the value of the materials, represented the least personal involvement on his part. Predictably, it also

131

produced the least response among the pupils, accounting for 16 loans on the seven occasions it was used or only 2.3 per activity.

Our predictions having been fulfilled, the premises set forth in our study were substantiated. Through correlation analyses, interviews with students, and comparison of the effectiveness of different teacher ploys we were able to see the influence of the teacher emerge supreme as the truly important reason students chose to use supplementary mathematics materials.

Conclusions. Regarding causality, our findings can be expressed in four points:

1. Teacher influence is the only one of three possible causal elements found to correlate in near significant fashion with the students' use of the media center. Therefore, it is the most tenable explanation of the reason why the students followed the teacher's suggestions and used the nonrequired supplementary materials.
2. A teacher viewed by his pupils as personable and/or knowledgeable is influential in that he can effect changes in the reading habits of his pupils without threat of punishment or promise of reward. The force of his appeal is dependent upon the degree of his personal involvement in it. The more he cares, the greater the student response.
3. There appears to be a relationship between the students' interest in the subject and their esteem and respect for the teacher. Teachers recognized as influential have pupils who are interested in the subject.
4. The use of the media center by students can be analyzed through a study of teacher characteristics as well as those of the students.

The Teacher and the Media Specialist—A Symbiotic Relationship

THE MATHEMATICS TEACHER AND THE SCHOOL MEDIA PROGRAM

All our efforts were expended to show that the teacher is the primary influence in the educational development of his students. This educational development consists of a host of learning activities both in and out of the classroom, among them being the use of media center or library materials. As the prime mover of the student, the teacher is an integral component of the school media center program, and it is sheer folly to plan a scheme for student involvement without considering this fact. In truth, teacher assistance is absolutely necessary for the media specialist to function with the assurance that all possible steps are being taken to promote optimum use. Briefly, the media specialist *needs* the teacher in order to perform effectively. Why then are mathematics materials not used in the majority of school media centers?

Neglect of mathematics media. Having witnessed the influence of a teacher in creating student users of library media, it made us wonder all the more about the established pattern of neglect so far as the subject of mathematics is concerned. We interviewed Mr. T at the close of the post-test, being especially interested in his impressions of the activity which he had just completed and the feasibility of such an effort on the part of any mathematics teacher.

Q1   Were you surprised at the results of the experiment?

A   Yes, I had never considered myself to be especially influential. The fact that the response was so great was surprising in view of the fact that the materials were not required.

Q2   Did you detect any difference in the two groups in their insight or understanding of the subject at the time of the study?

A   No, but the situation was purposely contrived to refrain from discussing the materials in class. I did not see any difference in test scores.

Q3   Were you surprised at the amount or quality of materials on the level of the pupils' ability?

A   Definitely, there is much more interesting and valuable material today than there was in the past.

Q4   Why didn't you do something like this before now?

A   I never really thought about it. Time is certainly a factor in preparing the bibliographies.

Q5   Would you do something like this in the future on your own initiative?

A   I am tempted to do so.

Q6   Why?

A   I think it is worthwhile. It provided the group with a variety of treatments and added insights. I would probably make it required work and would expect class presentations (oral reports) and would encourage discussion.

It is apparent that Mr. T has not had much contact with the media center in the past, and in this respect reflects a situation common to schools. The media specialist and the teacher of mathematics tend to know very little about each other's area of expertise; and in the pursuit of their respective functions rarely do their paths meet. We see this clearly in the recognition by Mr. T of the value of the undertaking but also a hesitancy to commit himself to a similar policy in the future. The time factor is his chief worry as indeed it would be to anybody who was unaware of the types of services which a school media center is designed to offer. Too few mathematics teachers know of the bibliographic function of media center service, and too few media specialists publicize this function to teachers of subjects found to be of minor user status.

This lack of professional contact or failure to communicate produces a neglect of the mathematics area in school media centers, for which representatives of both fields must share the responsibility. Of course, students are thus conditioned in the sense that they do not associate media center and library resources with the study of mathematics. Instead of cultivating the potential here, media specialists prefer to serve the needs of those teachers who operate in disciplines more familiar to them, such as English or social studies. Teachers in these fields are generally aware of the nature of media center services and tend to seek them out, while mathematics teachers tend to do without. The condition is comprehensible but no less *reprehensible.*

Methods of instruction—expository mode vs. inquiry. Of course, much of the blame for media center neglect must lie in the choice of teaching routines. Mathematics has been taught traditionally in the expository mode (designed for traditionally large groups) in which the teacher interprets the information to the student, the textbook being the essential source of information. Even at University High School, a truly innovative institution with relatively small classes, much energy was being expended (even during the conduct of our study) in developing a viable self-contained text.

There was a rather complete reliance on lectures, discussions, and in some cases, student reports, all directed toward predetermined goals set by the teacher. Our own instructional materials were selected and organized primarily to supplement the teacher's lectures in order to achieve the outcomes desired. Although beneficial under certain conditions, the expository approach tends to become self-defeating when a variety of learning experiences is recognized as highly desirable.

At present, there is a national trend toward greater flexibility within the classroom, and the curricula of teacher training institutions promulgate such thinking. They instill in the modern teacher the awareness that to facilitate the learning condition it may be necessary to organize students into several segments ranging from large groups to independent efforts. The approach used and the routines employed are based on the desired objectives and behaviors. In this way, the teacher is able to determine after careful consideration the optimum size of the group for each learning activity.

Along with the increased flexibility comes a new respect for the inquiry approach, sometimes called the discovery mode. In this operational pattern, the teacher serves as coordinator of discussion, organizer of materials, and manager of the learning enterprise. Rather than provide straight lecture, he establishes the conditions of learning so that the youngsters raise questions and seek out answers. This approach works well with small groups and resembles most nearly a research or problem-solving orientation since students develop and test hypotheses from which they can draw conclusions.

Obviously, such newer methods demand much of the teacher for which it is necessary that he be prepared. The media center and its resources take on greater significance in the learning environment because of the variety of experiences which they may be called upon to offer. The newly created teacher has an advantage in that he has been better educated in the function and utilization of library-based materials, and has developed a keener awareness of the role of the school media center. It remains for those of us who care to help the older teachers comprehend this as well.

The School Media Specialist and the Mathematics Program

We have seen the tremendous influence of an effective teacher in the educational life-style of his students. The teacher's power base is of such magnitude that we know that without his or her cooperation and assistance the media specialist cannot possibly hope to function at 100 percent level of efficiency. What about the media specialist, then, and his or her value to the mathematics program? That contribution is best understood through an attempt to answer the four vital questions raised by Knapp and enumerated in the first chapter:

1. What is the extent of the contribution to course work?
2. What is the nature of the contribution to the instructional program?
3. What factors limit the contribution to the instructional program?
4. What should be the contribution to the instructional program?

The media center's contribution to course work. In the field of mathematics there are great numbers of high quality materials which can and should be utilized. In addition to the trade books, film loops, filmstrips, and periodicals employed in our study, the interested educator is able to find concrete objects, games, motion pictures, programmed texts, study kits, and disc and tape recordings, to name just a few. These media cannot be effectively stored and disseminated in the mathematics classroom nor in the department office with any greater facility than is possible with any other discipline.

In addition, the use of these materials by students is only possible when the teacher knows of their existence. To be brought up to date and informed of new materials and their potential value is a great benefit to the improvement of one's instruction. To have a willing and able partner, a trained bibliographer no less, to help plan assignments and select pertinent media gives one the assurance that the best possible techniques are being employed utilizing the best possible instructional materials.

For this, a media specialist is needed, one who has become involved with the implementation of the curriculum and who is informed on departmental policies. It is absolutely necessary that the media specialist attend curriculum planning sessions and mathematics department meetings. Ideally, as we stated before, there would be a mathematics bibliography course common to the preparation of both teachers and school media people. This would help both parties gain the essential awareness of subject materials and also aid mathematics teachers develop a better understanding of the types of services a media center is designed to offer.

Nature of the contribution to the instructional program. The teacher in our study worked in an expository mode providing the option to his class of using library media to supplement his lectures and the basic text in achieving his objectives. This, of course, is only one form of enrichment activity. There is a myriad of other circumstances, routines, and designs for which use of the center may be incorporated. These range from *required* use involving the same expository approach in fulfillment of instructor-made goals to the less tightly structured practices utilized in the method of inquiry. As students become more independent of teacher prescriptions, the roles of the media center and the media specialist achieve increasing eminence, since the materials serve to heighten and augment rather than to merely supplement the learning situation.

Most important is the understanding that the media center is designed to support, enrich, and enhance the learning situation. Whether this involves guidance by the media specialist in a mathematics laboratory or bibliographic advice freely given to both students and teachers in a more traditional situation, the concept of friend and coworker must come through. As we have pointed out, it is doubtful that any media person can hope to achieve a level of influence equal to that of the teacher in the mind of the student. This is completely understandable in view of what we found in our study. What the media specialist must aspire to is the achievement of a similar level of influence with respect to bibliographic matters in the mind of the teacher.

That this is possible is seen in the results of our study which show a general consensus among students that mathematics materials were interesting and enjoyable, as well as informative. Film material especially was regarded as a recreational medium, one which was less taxing mentally than was a book. An astute teacher may exploit such sentiments to achieve stated behavioral objectives, and it is here that the media specialist can prove his or her worth. If students become interested in the array of learning experiences which the media specialist has helped to provide, it follows that they will become more receptive to the subject, and the learning environment is enhanced. This enables the teacher to function at a higher level of efficiency and increase his success overall. The general effect is that the teacher needs the media specialist as much as the teacher is needed by the media specialist—and this holds true for any teaching situation.

Factors limiting the contribution to the instructional program. In view of our findings, there is no factor limiting the contribution of the school media center to the instructional program in mathematics more than the failure of teachers and school media specialists to realize that their association is of mutual benefit. The lack of communication discussed with respect to the interview with Mr. T must be considered the greatest impediment to the development of a working relationship. For the students' sake, this situation cannot be suffered to continue for much longer. Instead, the two areas must come together and merge their talents in providing the best kinds of learning experiences. Make no mistake, media specialists must provide to mathematics teachers the same types of services as those received by teachers of English and social studies. In most cases this will necessitate an activist orientation on the part of the media specialist in initiating the necessary contact.

What the media center should contribute. This study has shown the type of contribution which can be made to the study of mathematics. Use of supplementary materials by pupils in optional tasks provides enrichment experiences judged by them to be interesting and enjoyable. Without a doubt, required reading and viewing will greatly aid the understanding of concepts and skills. Mr. T recognized as benefits accruing to student users added insights and new perspectives as a result of the variety of treatments afforded by different writers. His students in the experimental group changed their reading patterns dramatically in embracing the mathematics materials in the media center when they thought he considered it to be important.

In this way, mathematics was converted in the space of eight weeks from a minor user to a major user of the school media center. One great truth emerges from this: the school media center should contribute as much toward the realization of objectives and goals within a school's mathematics program as it does to any other discipline in the curriculum. Although certain teaching modes especially favor such a supportive role, the importance of the media center should manifest itself regardless of the methods and routines employed.

137

Overcoming the Barriers

That use of the media center by the students in our study did not last, once Mr. T ceased his involvement, indicates the degree to which the newly established milieu was dependent on his activity. The return to previously conditioned behavior was immediate, and it requires no great exercise in logic or imagination to comprehend it. Obviously, the mathematics teacher must consciously strive to utilize the full potential of media center resources, and the media specialist must be constant and dedicated to abetting the process. Only in this way is it possible to develop within students certain internalized values resulting in a new type of condition in which mathematics materials are considered as readily as are materials in social studies.

As we have already pointed out, there are numerous factors which militate against the fruition of a completely effective media center program. The close association of teachers and media specialists which we advocate requires a rather full understanding of each other's objectives and functions with respect to media center utilization. The unclear nature of the center's role is detrimental to the cooperative enterprise, and in the remaining pages we shall examine the obscurities and offer suggestions to eliminate them.

THE PRINCIPAL'S PART

In our study, we were fortunate that the principal was deeply interested in research and in his responsibility to the media center. He was dedicated to the adoption of any measure which he felt might improve the level of education at his school and gave full cooperation to our investigation. Without such a commitment on his part, our research could have been greatly hampered. It was obvious that his interest and enthusiasm were reflected in the receptive attitude to our task on the part of the mathematics department and the school media center.

Encouragement from above is fundamental to a successful media center operation, since the administrator is the chief catalyst in the establishment of working relationships among the professionals on his staff. If he does not fully understand the center's role, he must take it upon himself to learn as much as he can. He might begin by familiarizing himself with the new standards, *Media Programs: District and School*, and learn the basic principles of the unified media concept in discussions with media specialists, supervisors, and knowledgeable colleagues.

In preceding pages, we have alluded to the desirability of a mathematics bibliography course in the training of teachers and media specialists in preparing them for curriculum development. Although equally desirable for a school principal, it is even less likely to exist. Therefore, the principal ought to bring the professional staff together to discuss the various media which may be used successfully to meet certain teaching objectives. This can be a real learning experience for the conscientious administrator and he or she should make every effort to attend.

Also, it is necessary to observe media centers in action; one's own of course, and others, possibly less traditional, may serve as models for emulation. Visits to demonstration programs, mathematics laboratories, and resource centers are especially meaningful if the principal is accompanied by the school media specialist and representatives of the mathematics department. There will be great profit from this association in its provision of an opportunity for the parties to discuss the real problems involved in offering good media center service in mathematics.

This type of involvement helps establish the pattern for interpersonal relationships between teachers and media specialists necessary to the successful determination of teaching objectives and the place of the media center in instruction. Of course, the principal will include the media persons on all planning committees involving the mathematics curriculum, as he or she will require that the mathematics department be represented in any meeting or discussion regarding utilization of the media center. In this way the role of the media center is clarified and role conflicts tend to diminish.

Having done this, we can only hope that the principal continues to be an interested individual, encouraging teachers and media specialists to cooperate in providing a progressive program and keeping abreast of developments by attending library workshops and conferences. We may rightly feel that the principal has "arrived" who is able to conceptualize media center responsibilities contained within curriculum reforms such as team teaching, flexible scheduling, and individualization of instruction. In such an eventuality, we have a competent authority to promulgate the important role of the school media center.

COMMUNICATIONS

We have already singled out the lack of interpersonal communication between mathematics teachers and school media specialists as the most serious limitation in the development of a good working relationship. In our description of the principal we found what a strong influence he can be in helping to overcome such conditions by providing the right kind of encouragement and support. Nevertheless, it is still up to the practicing professionals to determine to what degree they will work in concert.

Probably it will be necessary for the media specialist to initiate the contact, since the mathematics teacher has "functioned" for a long time without his or her help. Clearly, the involvement of the teacher requires a great deal of extra effort on his or her part, and the principal's encouragement should be accompanied by an active concern on the part of the media specialist. The desirable quality here is true empathy for the teacher's role, an interest which we hope is derived from experience in teaching (although not necessarily mathematics). It has been shown that media specialists with classroom experience have less trouble in establishing rapport with faculty members.

Without doubt, personal contact is highly superior to written requests or invitations to come to the media center and make any curricular needs known. Such announcements find their way to an almost final resting place in the circular file immediately upon receipt, since they approximate closely the image of bulk mail. Care and understanding are best expressed in a direct conversational mode where uncertainties are clarified and suggestions easily rendered.

For the media center to function at its highest level, teachers must also cooperate in keeping the channels of communication open. The media specialist's efforts to provide and make available the diversity and range of media that can help teachers and students reach desired curricular goals are wasted when the teachers do not avail themselves of the media center's resources—material and human. The media specialist is a member of the teaching team whose effectiveness depends in great part on the other team members.

We have discussed the necessity of joint attendance at faculty and media center meetings to set a pattern for subsequent cooperation. Both parties should as a matter of routine keep each other informed of the appearance of new materials and implementation of new policies. When this is done in a friendly, natural, and easy manner, whether in scheduled conferences or informal conversation, the results will be beneficial and create the necessary interface.

It is especially important that the media specialist reach the new teachers, not only to be friendly, but also to let them know there is available to them professional service and expertise. The receptive attitude, the open mind, the sincere interest, when joined with a real awareness of curricular needs will help sell to the teaching staff the idea of media center involvement. Future generations of students will reap the rewards.

CURRICULUM DEVELOPMENT AND IMPLEMENTATION

In developing and implementing the curriculum it is essential that both media specialist and mathematics teacher share basic understandings. The mathematics bibliography course covering all media would be extremely valuable as a common experience in their preparation; and educators from both fields should take heed. Practicing professionals would do well to consider taking such a course if at all possible. Also important is an understanding of curriculum theory and design which may best be examined in further formal coursework. The school media center will then achieve a solid foundation based on the needs of the mathematics instructional program. Let us examine some of the ways in which this may be accomplished.

Preplanned visits. One of the most rewarding activities is the classroom visit to the media center; however, it may also prove to be the most disastrous of occurrences if not properly prepared. The teacher must inform the media specialist of the nature of the unit of study well beforehand and should seek suggestions for optimum utilization of available materials. Such cooperative planning helps to identify for both parties the desired objectives and permits the necessary evaluation of the outcomes of the activity.

These visits provide many opportunities for learning to take place, therefore the media person can wear many hats. For example, he or she may provide guidance to the students in selection and use of materials, instruct them in direct fashion in reading and library skills peculiar to mathematics, and even serve along with the teacher as an interpreter of information. With a clear idea of the teacher's expectations, the media specialist knows precisely what role to play and thereby diminishes the possibility of role conflict. Given these circumstances, the visits ought to prove of value and mathematics teachers will become more interested in the media center's resources.

Selection of unit materials and choice of assignments. The media specialist can be a real asset to the teacher in implementing the curriculum if he or she is both knowledgeable of learning theory and committed to a multimedia program. An understanding of teaching methodology together with a thorough familiarity of the center's math holdings places the media professional in a unique position to show teachers how good materials are beneficial in developing certain student behaviors. With this knowledge, he or she can provide a big assist in suggesting additional topics for study as well as techniques to develop them.

Of course, the teacher must keep the media specialist informed of the abilities and interests of the students and, as well, the existence of especially difficult problems in motivation. The good media person may be able to help surmount such obstacles with his or her awareness of alternate sources and related tools, being indeed the bridge needed by the teacher to assure optimum use of available media and as such willing to provide sound advice and judgment to accomplish this.

Here, again, cooperative effort is the indispensable element, and much of the bibliographic endeavor must be regarded as a joint activity. Earlier in the study we pointed to the naivete of mathematics teachers regarding library services. Whenever possible, teachers and media specialists, together, should examine the collection and decide what books, films, tapes, or chapters and sections thereof are meaningful to specific study units. The outcome may well be a precise, functional bibliography of available works on the subject, one for which the teacher may take at least partial credit. In this way, the teacher develops the library awareness which we so desire.

Instructional responsibilities. We have already shown the teacher to be the direct link between the student and his attempts at curriculum-related activities. Even though the media specialist has a secondary position as manifested in direct instruction, there are things that he or she can accomplish. Some of these were mentioned in the foregoing discussion of planned visits when we pointed out the media person's multifaceted role. Success here requires the full support of the teacher.

A natural for the mathematics program is the conduct of team teaching sessions in the background and history of the discipline. These are structured primarily for the purpose of arousing interest and stimulating further efforts, and therefore both media persons and teachers would be well advised to studiously avoid the humdrum lecture but attempt to involve students in an active manner. Employing a discovery approach with proper utilization of effective media, these sessions may serve either to introduce the students to a new unit of study, or to culminate their involvement with a unit just completed. These sessions are better handled in the media center where fundamental research techniques may be taught along with certain library skills peculiar to mathematics. The students are then enabled to find answers and solutions utilizing the mathematics materials of diverse nature.

Similar to this with respect to direct instructional responsibilities is the provision of media talks as a regular teaching routine. Interesting episodes, monumental achievements, serious setbacks—all representative of human endeavor and drawn from available literature—can be made part of the learning experience. When students see their teacher participate actively with the media specialist in such activities, they will tend to develop a healthy interest in his or her identity as a helpful individual. Alternative techniques include panel discussions, forums, and role playing, in which the youngsters are expected to share their learning with fellow students. The possibilities are endless.

One more point which we should not overlook is the responsibility of the media specialist to teach teachers in the use of the other media. Many teachers will shy away from the use of film and tapes simply because they are unaware of how to set up the equipment. It is up to the media specialist, with the solid support of the principal, to set up workshops or in-service sessions at convenient times for members of the faculty.

Of great benefit to the mathematics teacher is the capacity to make his own materials for classroom use. It may well be that he or she has some good ideas for achieving certain results but has been frustrated by a lack of available media. The good media person will first learn of this felt need by establishing the correct interface, then act upon it by taking the teacher aside and showing him or her how to create transparencies, tapes, or slides which could enable him to perform in a more efficient manner.

Such lessons conducted in response to personal felt needs are best held in private and should be a continuous service of the school media program. In this manner, supplementary materials are utilized most productively and gain new adherents among members of the faculty. Teachers then transfer this enthusiasm to their students who ultimately become media center and library users.

Individualized instruction and independent study. Our discussion of curriculum development has centered on what we may term a traditional instructional approach, since this was the manner in which Mr. T's classes were handled. At present, however, there is a decided shift in thinking away from certain principles of group dynamics toward the individual and his right to learn at his own pace in his own way, regardless of what the "average pupil" is doing.

Such a program mandates the highest degree of cooperative planning between the teacher and all available human resources including the student, himself. Skills, concepts, and topics are decided upon and arranged in sequence and, based on a knowledge of entering behaviors, each student is given a personalized program for achievement which he or she pursues in an independent fashion.

As before, the teacher is the essential ingredient, but with a somewhat changed role. Mr. T, in our study, served as the information source from which the students derived their basic understanding. Had he been operating within an individualized program, he would have been more a manager of the learning process, identifying, arranging, and organizing the necessary strategies and materials and later evaluating student performance.

To the teacher involved in an individualized program, there is no educational aide more valuable than the school media specialist, simply because the crucial factor to success lies in the provision of suitable materials in sufficient quantity. Organizing these materials for use is possibly the most taxing and time-consuming activity, and in the media person the teacher finds the expertise which is absolutely necessary. The teacher is then in a position to make valid decisions based not only upon an awareness of a student's needs but also upon awareness of available resources.

Again, the media person and the teacher are operating as a team doing the kinds of things previously described, such as planning projects and class visits and selecting topics and materials. The media specialist takes his turn, along with the teacher, in acting as guide, interpreter, or coordinator as the occasion demands, while the teacher provides assistance in the teaching of media center skills. If the teacher consciously motivates students to use such resources, it is close to an ironclad guarantee that the media center will come into much wider use.

This concept of independent effort is especially realistic when dealing with bright students such as those in our study. These youngsters worked well with little direction from above since they were motivated largely by their own sense of responsibility. It certainly would have benefitted the members of our experimental group who were cognizant of the value of supplementary material but had precious little time to visit the media center. Had we been able to implement a program based on the discovery approach in which students were encouraged to seek out information on their own, using the materials available in the media center, or even a specially designated mathematics laboratory, most likely the results of the study would have been truly impressive.

BOOK SELECTION AND COLLECTION BUILDING

Along with curriculum development is the equally important task of developing the collection. Although, traditionally this has been the media specialist's responsibility (much as the ultimate choice of curricular techniques belongs to the teacher), it is an activity which should be shared. To be sure, the media person has a better concept of the breadth of the total curriculum, but he or she needs the depth of understanding provided by the mathematics teacher when ordering materials in the discipline.

Joint participation in book selection generally serves as an indicator of a healthy school media center program, since teachers who are partially responsible for the holdings are in a fortunate position to encourage student use. Of course, both parties need to be informed and a good practice would be for them to search together the bibliographic tools, discuss the possible choices, and order what both agree to be useful.

There is little chance for conflict here since the media specialist is interested in building the best collection possible and in enlisting the teacher's support in the enterprise. If a dispute does arise, however, we do feel that in the best interest of the school both parties must agree that the media professional has the final word. The media center's collection building is that staff member's responsibility, and only he or she is authorized to make purchases for it. Bibliography is the media specialist's area of expertise, one for which he or she has been educated in certain valid principles. Keeping in mind that the media person is endeavoring to build strength and overcome deficiencies of the collection as a whole with relatively small funding should allay the suspicion of a reasonable mathematics teacher that his or her personal desires are being given short shrift. At least we hope so.

Finally, there is the matter of textbook selection which is the peculiar province of the faculty member. Again, this task should be shared with the library media professional. We hope that in his or her wisdom the enlightened principal will appoint the media specialist to the textbook committee, if one exists, since he or she possesses a knowledge of publishers and selection tools and can provide input which is valuable in the final consideration.

The literature is replete with suggestions as to the manner by which teachers and media center personnel should engage in bibliographic pursuits. These range from the formally scheduled departmental meetings or individual conferences held by the media specialist with every teacher to loosely structured afternoon book teas in which all teachers are invited to the center for refreshments and discussions of suitable materials for their programs. In whatever way it is approached, it is important for the media specialist to make a special effort in the case of mathematics teachers, since in most instances the desired interface is totally lacking in precedent.

COMMUNITY RELATIONS

The final consideration concerns the media person as a liaison with the community, much as is the principal of the school. The principal's objectives, however, lie primarily within the realm of organizational and supervisory functions (seeing that the school maintains a favorable reputation as a community agency) while the media specialist can be a bit more "selfish" in outlook. He or she is interested in the development of an outstanding educational program and therefore will seek to cultivate those individuals, societies, agencies, and organizations which may help to further this end.

Every prospective school media specialist is taught the value of a human resources file, but it is a great pity that these are rarely structured to benefit the mathematics program. Most frequently we have on record the names of individuals who are willing to give time to discuss problems or trends in such areas as business, accounting, political science, and civics.

Also we have our share of linguists, historians, artists, musicians, and even physical culturists. Mathematics programs generally go unnoticed in this quest for outside expertise, when in reality many of these same individuals could provide such classes with a tremendous source of enrichment.

Artists and musicians might be prevailed upon to discuss the influence of mathematics in the concept, design, and structure of their fields. A businessman might well talk about the type of mathematical awareness which is indispensable to his operation. The media specialist is able to contact the personnel departments of large industries in the area to put him or her in touch with engineers, designers, or architects who might be willing to serve as resource people for individual student projects as well.

Of course, any related professional organization and institution of higher education in the vicinity represents sources of brain power which on the whole are receptive to the requests of duly authorized representatives of local schools. These also make good sources of materials for students to utilize in developing their topics or seeking answers to questions posed in class. Some well-placed phone calls from the media specialist may serve to open the door for students to use such institutional materials. It may even result in some gifts to the school media center.

Certainly, it is necessary for teachers and media people to discuss the need for help of this kind before it is possible to frame a request. After this has been done and the units of study planned in such a way that the media specialist understands what is expected of the outside resources, he or she is in a position to initiate contacts with definite goals in mind. In short, it must become apparent that the mathematics program like any other curricular offering has a valid claim to all the expertise and available assistance which a community can muster. It is just as certain that media specialists and teachers must work hard in order to establish the claim.

Epilogue

Once a researcher finishes his investigation, he immediately begins to meditate on what he might have done differently. Much like life itself, the completion of a scholarly study leads to a series of afterthoughts which, given the time and energy, one may choose to pursue at a later date. Doctoral candidates are given the opportunity to reflect on this in the final section of their dissertation usually entitled "Suggestions for Further Research."

Certainly, this investigator is no different and as the reader may have surmised by the several allusions provided in the text, his original study concluded on that note. One of these suggestions was to replicate at an average public school. Another involved the use of three groups taught by

146

the same teacher, one getting the experimental group treatment, the second getting the treatment from the media specialist, and the third being the control. This in effect would serve to discriminate between the effects of bibliographic guidance provided by the librarian and those related to teacher influence. Other suggestions involved long-term projects and large-scale efforts.

In expanding the scope of the dissertation and writing this book, however, these recommendations have assumed a less important character. It is now more essential that broad meaningful concepts are better understood by the practicing professionals, rather than that the original research be substantiated or vindicated by subsequent experimenters. If we have made a contribution to the development of viable library-media center programs in the mathematics curriculum by helping teachers, media specialists, and principals conceptualize their roles, this is reward enough.

The teacher who is aware of the existence and availability of media center resources and services, cognizant of his responsibilities in developing in his students an interest in the subject as well as a mastery of skills, and who in turn is highly regarded by the students is the key to the pupils' use of the media center in a self-initiated manner. When joined by an enthusiastic and knowledgeable media specialist and encouraged by an enlightened school administrator, the necessary ingredients are present.

By necessity, this study was limited to the parameters we chose to incorporate. In truth, it is only a small part of the total library contribution, and should be considered little more than a starting point for the development of new or yet untried activities. The innovative school staff should be constant in their attempts to better the existing situation. It is our fervent hope that we have provided the stimulus for experimentation in an area which is challenging albeit somewhat frustrating. Only in this way, will we ever realize the full potential of the school media center in the mathematics program.

Appendix A

Necessary Teacher Qualities and Requirements

Required of the mathematics teacher is:

1) A willingness to participate in a study in which one of his classes would be affected for about eight weeks in order to determine his influence on their use of library materials and

   a) to help investigator select books for mention to the experimental group in relation to coverage of subject matter, as well as
   b) to allow investigator's presence in class for both control and experimental groups

2) Competence in subject field

3) Experience (enough to determine in advance the approximate coverage of the eight week period)

4) Presence on the job during the summer session in order to meet with the investigator

5) Assignment of two classes of the same level for the fall term

6) Personable nature and good rapport with pupils

7) If not a belief in the value of the library for mathematics, an open mind on the subject.

Important considerations in the selection of the participating teacher presented to the Head of the Mathematics Department, University High School, prior to undertaking the study.

Questionnaire to Registrants of UICSM Summer Institute

To: Mathematics Institute Participant

During the fall term an experiment will be conducted at University High School using the subfreshmen (junior high level) math classes. It will attempt to examine the influence of a mathematics teacher on his students' use of non-required library materials. We are asking your help with regard to two aspects of the study.

I. *Recommended books or magazine articles*

Please list any books or articles which you feel to be appropriate and rewarding as supplementary materials for this age group. These may be textbooks of various levels for purposes of clarification of method, presentation of alternative views or approaches, or advanced work for honor students, recreational, historical, biographical, or fictional material for enjoyment and enrichment, source books and popularizations for general knowledge, etc.

Author	Title	Why Recommended
1.		
2.		
3.		
4.		
5.		

II. *Reasons for use of materials*

On the basis of your own experiences in the field, please cite as many possible reasons as you can for math students following teacher suggestions for reading nonrequired material.
1.
2.
3.
4.
5.

Weekly Bibliographies

Mathematics Bibliography (Oct. 20-24)

Abbot, Edwin. *Flatland: A Romance of Many Dimensions*, pp. 53–63.

In this classic imaginative tale you are taken on a fascinating journey by a citizen of Flatland to a land of lines and points. Especially interesting and informative are Sections 13 and 14 of Part II, "How I Had a Vision of Lineland" and "How I Vainly Tried to Explain the Nature of Flatland." You will enjoy the conversation between the King of Lineland and the Flatlander, and in doing so will probably gain a greater understanding of lines and points.

Lieber, Lillian. *The Education of T. C. Mits*, pp. 43–50, 74–80.

If you have not seen this interesting little mathematical piece before this, you should read Chapter 4 "Generalization" and Chapter 7 "Abstraction" which deal with algebra and geometry. In Chapter 7 the point is treated briefly and in clear fashion. You will greatly enjoy the poetic style of the author.

Rogers, James T. *The Pantheon Story of Mathematics for Young People*.

A good readable text and fine illustrations trace the history of math from finger counting to modern ideas. You will gain an appreciation of mathematical development by skimming through the whole book and looking at all the pictures. Of most interest are Chapters 1 and 2 concerning the Egyptians and Babylonians and Chapter 4 on the Greeks.

Vergara, William. *Mathematics In Everyday Things*, pp. 82–83.

This book relates the principles of mathematics to everyday objects and occurrences. Of interest to you at this time is the interesting little description of Galileo's rationale in proposing that lines have an infinite number of points. Although you may not fully understand his line of reasoning,

These bibliographies were compiled by the investigator with the help and approval of the teacher. They were pertinent to material covered in class and distributed to pupils on a week to week basis as part of the teaching "routine."

you will appreciate the fact that this was a departure from the geometry of Euclid and led to the study of calculus.

PERIODICAL ARTICLE

Gogan, Daisy. "A Game With Shapes" *Arithmetic Teacher* 16:283–84 (April 1969).
This is a delightful little game which you can learn to play with your friends. At first it looks simple but it may present a challenge to you.

FILMSTRIP

"Distance and Betweenness," SVE Films A542-1.
You should examine this filmstrip carefully either by yourself or with a friend in order to discuss the concepts of segments, rays, points, lines, and planes as presented. It will provide a valuable experience in helping you to understand these ideas.

Mathematics Bibliography (Oct. 27–31)

Here is another bibliography of materials which I strongly recommend you use because these items will help you understand math concepts and also give you background information which you will not find anywhere else in our study. The titles are on reserve in the library and I hope everybody can examine one, or two, or three, or all of them. Happy reading time!

Mr. T

Gardner, Martin. *Mathematics, Magic, and Mystery*, pp. 114–17.
This little book contains 115 different diversions and recreations which will challenge your abilities. At this time, you will enjoy doing the problem called "Line Paradox" in chapter 7. How does the line vanish? The answer is easy enough but it's fun to consider.

Muir, Jane. *Of Men and Numbers*, pp. 1–25.
The opening pages of this book contain the stories of three great mathematicians of Ancient Greece. You will enjoy and profit in reading of the contributions of Pythagoras, Euclid, and Archimedes whose work will soon be familiar to you. What influence they had on the development of mathematics is explained in an easy-to-understand manner. This should be read by every pupil whether or not he likes mathematics.

Sharp, Evelyn. *A New Mathematics Reader*, pp. 43–54.

Last week we discussed some of the different types of numbers and this book has an especially good section on the number system. Rationals, irrationals, and naturals are explained in clear fashion. All kinds of mathematical concepts which you encounter in school are covered and you may want to read further.

Ward, Morgan and C. Hardgrove. *Modern Elementary Mathematics*, pp. 177–78, 185.

Although this book was written for teachers you will find it easy to understand pages 177–78, "Geometric Objects Considered as Point Sets," in which lines, line segments, and rays are explained. Mathematical symbols are identified here, and also on page 185 which deals with congruence. You will find it helpful.

PERIODICAL ARTICLE

Bardis, Panos. "Evolution of Pi: An Essay in Mathematical Progress from the Great Pyramid to Eniac," *School Science and Mathematics* 60: 73–78 (January 1960).

This is a fine historical description of the evaluations of Pi, covering those made in China, Japan, India, Babylonia, Greece, and modern nations. You will recall our discussion last week regarding the value of Pi and now you will better understand why any value can only be an approximate value.

FILM CONCEPT LOOP

"Motion Geometry," Macmillan MGA1.

If you have never used a film loop before you will like this one. It shows a white figure and the different positions it takes when slides, flips, and turns are applied. Each type of movement is shown by a different color. See if you can guess the meaning of red, green, and yellow colors.

Mathematics Bibliography (Nov. 3–7)

This bibliography will serve as a good introduction to the study of angles which will be our next topic in motion geometry. I have carefully chosen these titles and hope that *everybody* makes it a point to use them.

Mr. T

Bakst, Aaron. *Mathematics, Its Magic and Mastery*, pp. 494–96.

There is a wealth of material about mathematics presented in this large book. Don't be afraid of its size, however, since the excellent section, "Tailoring with Straight Lines and Angles," is only two pages long. It serves as a good introduction to the study of angles.

Fowler, H. Waller. *Kites*, pp. 9–16.

You may be interested to know that kites were used in Asia centuries ago. The first chapter, "History of the Kite," describes the development and use of kites through the ages. The second chapter, "Theories of Kite Flying," describes the angle effects in construction. You will like this one.

Hogben, Lancelot. *Wonderful World of Mathematics*, pp. 15–17.

Of all the math books written for youngsters, this is one of the best. Be sure to see the section on "Taxes and Triangles" for an excellent description of the Egyptians' use of right angle measure in construction. When you come to a word which is followed by a picture of a hand, it means you can look it up in the glossary at the back of the book.

MacLean, W. B. *Mathematics—Grade 7*, pp. 265–69.

This is a fine text which you may wish to examine at length. The section, "Measuring Angles Using a Protractor," provides you with a first experience in this area. Since we will be doing a great deal of work with protractors, you can get a head start here. At the back of the book there is a protractor that you can use for practice.

PERIODICAL ARTICLE

Allen, Bruce. "Patterns of Intersection," *Arithmetic Teacher* 15:560–61 (October 1968).

This is a brief but interesting article on the various ways that an eighth grade class used intersecting lines to form patterns. Also, they discovered something about the angles that were formed. Try their experiment for yourself.

FILMSTRIP

"Angles," SVE A542-3.

This filmstrip contains straightforward definitions and a great deal of information on angles. Don't worry if you can't understand all of it—if you make an attempt you will be ahead of the rest of us. Stop when you come to the section on dihedral angles since they are of no interest to us at this time.

Mathematics Bibliography (Nov. 10–14)

Here are some more titles which will help you in your study of angles. I recommend them highly and feel that any time spent in examining these library materials is time well-spent.

Mr. T

Adler, Irving. *The Giant Golden Book of Mathematics*, pp. 23, 27.
This is another of the really good math books for youngsters. It is colorful, easy to read, and enjoyable but still contains much useful information. Especially helpful to you at this time are the sections, "Right Angle" on page 23 and "Equal Sides and Equal Angles" on page 27.

Bell, Stuart E. *Rotation and Angles* (Mathematics in the Making #4),
This small 32-page pamphlet-style item will prove to be one of the most helpful titles you have read for this class. It will not take long for you to read through the whole item since there are many illustrations and diagrams. Most important, you will learn a great deal from the bright and pleasant pages.

Crown, A. W. *The Language of Triangles*, vol. 1, pp. 1–4.
This book was written for a high school trigonometry class but you will profit from reading the first few pages dealing with the history of triangles. In this section, many notable figures such as Thales, Hipparchus, Hero, and our old friend, Pythagoras, are mentioned. You will also find out about such terms as tangent and cosine.

Fadiman, Clifton. *Fantasia Mathematica*, pp. 35–36.
This is an interesting and amusing collection of stories and diversions which you will truly enjoy. You will like especially the little imaginary tale of "Pythagoras and the Psychoanalyst" in which the great mathematician seeks advice concerning his passion for drawing triangles. His problem is handled so well that the Pythagorean theorem is never discovered. Your parents would like this one also.

Periodical article

Sandling, D. C. "Plane Polygons," *Arithmetic Teacher* 11:569–70 (December 1964).
This article describes the way a math class used a clock to illustrate different types of angles. Also, you will find out what a polygon is and how the names of different kinds of polygons were determined.

FILMSTRIP
"Congruent Figures," Eyegate Films 186-H.
You will learn a great deal about the congruence of angles from this informative filmstrip. Also, you will find out something about the characteristics of triangles and other figures. You will be familiar with some of the information but don't worry if you aren't able to comprehend all of it.

Mathematics Bibliography (Nov. 17–21)

Since we will be concluding our study of angles this week, I have provided you with what I consider to be a list of fine library materials on symmetry. This will be our next topic in motion geometry and can be understood much more easily if you read these items. Please do so.

Mr. T

Bell, Stuart. *Transformations and Symmetry* (Mathematics in the Making #7).
Here is another of those interesting, colorful, and informative 32-page pamphlets by Mr. Bell. You will find out about lines of symmetry or mirror lines. How does this fit in with what you know about flip lines? Planes of symmetry and order of symmetry are also covered. If you look through this item, you will profit a great deal. Be sure to see it.

Johnson, Donovan A. *Paper Folding for the Mathematics Class*, pp. 18–19.
After our experience in paper folding last week, you will want to get this booklet. Those who like to make designs and models will be especially interested. The two-page section on symmetry contains four examples of paper folds which help illustrate what we are doing in math; "Line Symmetry," "Line and Point Symmetry," "Synthetical Design," and "Snowflake Pattern." Try one or two and enjoy yourself.

Ravielli, Anthony. *An Adventure in Geometry*, pp. 13–26.
It will not take you more than a few minutes to read the first part of this beautifully illustrated book which deals with "Design in Nature." In these few pages, you will learn much about the concept of symmetry (although you probably won't be able to resist reading further). I feel that this is one of the best books for math students and would like all of you to see it.

Weyl, Hermann. *Symmetry* (skim whole book).
This is a stimulating and well-written description of the concept of

symmetry. You need not read any of the pages but please look at the pictures to discover the use of symmetry in art and nature as well as mathematics.

PERIODICAL ARTICLE

Miller, J. E. "Symmetry in Nature," *Arts and Activities* 45:40–41 (September 1967).
Written by an art teacher, this very brief article will help you to understand the importance of symmetry. Also you will encounter the term, "asymmetry." What does this word mean to you?

FILM CONCEPT LOOP

"Motion Geometry," Macmillan MGA 2.
Here is another film about that little white element. This time, see what happens when two flip lines are introduced and the second one is turned. Does the white element then travel round in a circle? How does a turn relate to a flip? You will enjoy this one.

Mathematics Bibliography (Nov. 24–28)

Since this is Thanksgiving Week and you will have two days to enjoy yourselves, I have provided you with a list of materials which you can finish easily before vacation. I hope that everybody makes an effort to get to the library to use these excellent items on symmetry.

Mr. T

Bergamini, David. *Mathematics*, pp. 88–97.
Beautifully illustrated with little text, these few pages on "Mathematics of Beauty in Nature and Art" will please and delight you. Especially interesting is the description of nature's spirals (shells and flowers). Also, you will find out about the Golden Rectangle and what it means to art and architecture. Don't miss this one.

Gardner, Martin. *The Ambidextrous Universe*, pp. 7–14.
Chapter Two, "Lineland and Flatland," is an entertaining and informative section in which you will learn many interesting things about symmetry. How do you use a mirror to determine if a figure is symmetrical or not? Which of the capital letters are symmetric? Put this one high up on your list.

Gardner, Martin. *The Scientific American Book of Mathematical Puzzles and Diversions*, pp. 162–69.

Another fine book by Mr. Gardner is this one in which he presents an interesting discussion of different types of symmetry such as musical reflection and palindromic sentences. Can you think of any words that are asymmetric when printed horizontally but acquire a line of symmetry when printed vertically? You will have fun with this one.

Payne, Joseph. *Harbrace Mathematics 7*, pp. 201–4.

This is a good seventh grade textbook to read and you will find the section on symmetry helpful to your understanding of the concept. Although we shall not be going into planes of symmetry as yet, it is a good idea to find out what the terms mean. It will be good practice for you to do numbers 1, 2, and 3 of the Exercises on pages 203–204. I suggest that you all look at this book.

PERIODICAL ARTICLE

Walter, Marion. "Some Mathematical Ideas Involved in the Mirror Cards," *Arithmetic Teacher* 14:115–24 (February 1967).

This is a fine informative article which should help you understand the concepts involved in mirror images. Pages 119–124 contain an especially helpful presentation of lines of symmetry. We may have some mirror cards in the math office that interested people might borrow.

FILMSTRIP

"Bisecting Angles and Segments," Eyegate Films 186-I.

This is a good review of many things that you already know concerning congruences and angles, but it will also provide some new information. See what happens when a kite is divided into sections by what is called the angle bisector. What is a quadrilateral? This filmstrip will also help you to understand the material on our next topic in motion geometry, "Perpendiculars and Parallels."

Mathematics Bibliography (Dec. 1–5)

Now that your holiday is over and you are anxious to get back to work, here is a list of materials which will help you do just that. Our new topic in motion geometry deals in perpendiculars and parallels and these fine titles will help you to achieve a complete understanding. Please get up to the library and use them this week.

Mr. T

Bendick, Jeanne. *Take Shapes, Lines, and Letters*, pp. 12–15.

This is an interesting and easily understood math book from which you will profit. It is a joy to read with many interesting pictures to help illustrate the concepts and you may want to read much further than the sections on "Parallel Lines" and "Angles." I am sure you will like this one and I hope you don't overlook it.

Court, Nathan. *Mathematics in Fun and Earnest*, pp. 117–18.

You will enjoy many of the fine essays in this book, but for this week it is recommended that you read only the very brief "Parallelism in Euclid's Elements." In what ways is parallelism part of our everyday life? Why is this theorem regarded as one of Euclid's clumsiest expressions? Find out for yourself.

Neely, Henry. *Triangles: Getting Ready for Trigonometry*, pp. 45–47.

Although this book deals primarily with the history and uses of triangles, the section, "Right, Vertical, and Perpendicular," is of great interest to our present study. What does the term, "right," mean and from where did it come? "Perpendicular" also has an interesting origin as does "vertical" and its parent word, "vertex." Many of you are interested in word origins and will be especially interested.

Paling, D. *Making Mathematics: A Secondary Course 2*, pp. 47–49.

This is a very fine English math text which contains a great deal of information while being inviting and easy to read. The section on "Lines and Points" provides you with several helpful exercises. With tracing paper and ruler, you can acquire a mastery of the concepts of perpendiculars and parallels. Don't pass this one up.

PERIODICAL ARTICLE

Ray, William J. "Just for Fun: From Arc to Time and Time to Arc," *Arithmetic Teacher* 14:671–73 (December 1967).

This article contains an excellent discussion of time and the relationship of hours to meridians of the earth. It's fun to figure out "how many degrees you are" from other areas of the world, and by doing this, figure out what time it is in those places.

FILMSTRIP

"Segments and Polygons," Eyegate Films 186-G.

The first half of this filmstrip is especially helpful covering the concepts

159

of perpendiculars, parallels, and symmetric relationships. The second part of the filmstrip deals with different types of polygons, and may be covered at a faster rate. I am sure you will benefit from this item and I recommend that you make it a point to see it.

Mathematics Bibliography (Dec. 8–12)

Since our next topic in motion geometry deals with triangles, I have taken the necessary steps in providing you with what I consider to be a list of good materials on the subject. I know that you will profit from your trip to the library and I hope that everybody sees these items.

Mr. T

Anderson, Raymond. *Romping Through Mathematics*, pp. 33–36.
This easy-to-read and informative book will provide you with a great deal of historical information. In the chapter, "Egyptian Rope Swingers," you will learn how the ancient Egyptians developed the idea of bisecting the angle and for what reason they did so. Although you are asked to read only the first few pages, you will probably want to read further in the chapter.

Experiences in Mathematical Discovery—Geometry, pp. 51–52, 59–60, 65–66.
The fourth volume of this interesting and valuable set concerns geometry and contains much useful information on triangles. I ask that you read two pages from each of three sections; "Angles of a Triangle," "Sides of a Triangle," and "Right Triangle." The problems and exercises will help you gain a greater understanding of the concepts. Be sure to see it.

Heafford, Phillip. *The Math Entertainer*, p. 20.
You will really enjoy this little book of teasers, tricks, and tests designed to bring out your best efforts in meeting the challenges. Find out how much you know about triangles by taking "The Triangle Test." You might have to take a smart classmate with you to help, and even then you probably won't get all ten answers correct. You will have fun with this one.

Kline and Crown. *The Language of Shapes*, pp. 61–66.
Chapter 10, "Triangle Shapes and Their Names," is just great since you will discover the names and characteristics of various kinds of triangles. What type of triangle has all three sides of different lengths? Which triangle has two equal sides? How big are the angles of an equilateral

triangle? The exercises on page 64 are also a challenge and you might want to try them. I recommend this one highly.

Periodical Article

Phillips, Jo. "Jo Phillips on Symmetries," *Instructor* 76:86–87+ (December 1966).

With the Christmas season fast approaching, you will especially enjoy this interesting article by a member of the University High School faculty. Using Christmas tree ornaments as examples, Mrs. Phillips explains line, point, and plane symmetry of various patterns. You will learn more about design and also might get some ideas for projects of your own.

Filmstrip

"Congruence," SVE Films A542–4.

You should not have any trouble understanding this filmstrip. The congruence of triangles is covered in a manner which should be quite clear to you. Different examples of congruent triangles are presented and you will gain a deeper comprehension of this concept. It is certainly worth your time to see it and I hope that everybody does.

Rating Scale

Directions: This is probably the first time you have seen a rating scale. It is completed by selecting any of the five numbers to answer the questions. Choose carefully and circle the number which best describes how you feel. Number one (1) is the lowest rating while number five (5) is the highest. You may use the same number to describe more than one item.

1. List each of your major subject teachers in the first column and rate each of them on the two characteristics of Good Teaching and Personality.

Teachers	Good teaching—Knows the subject well, and gets students to understand it					Personality—Is helpful, friendly, non-threatening, and generally likeable				
_____	1	2	3	4	5	1	2	3	4	5
_____	1	2	3	4	5	1	2	3	4	5
_____	1	2	3	4	5	1	2	3	4	5
_____	1	2	3	4	5	1	2	3	4	5
_____	1	2	3	4	5	1	2	3	4	5

2. Rate the major subjects you are now taking according to your interest in them. High interest (5) might be shown by your willingness to take extra courses in the subject, major in it in college or teach or work in it as an adult. Low interest (1) would mean you would just like to pass the course and then forget about it.

Social Studies	1	2	3	4	5
English	1	2	3	4	5
Math	1	2	3	4	5
Science	1	2	3	4	5
Latin	1	2	3	4	5

The rating scale was given to members of both the control and experimental groups of pupils at University High School.

Interview Questions— Experimental Group

Since I observed you in your math class, let's talk primarily about math.

1. Why do you think Mr. T spent so much time talking about math books?

2. Do you think he was right or wrong? Why?

3a. I notice that you used math library materials on (at least two) (several) (many) occasions. What do you think is the main reason you used them more than once?

3b. I notice that you used math library materials on only one occasion. Why not more often?

3c. I notice that you didn't use math library materials at all. Don't you usually follow a teacher's recommendations? Why not this time with Mr. T?
   (If question 3c applies, go to question 7.)

4. Were you satisfied with the library materials or somewhat disappointed? Why?

5. Were you always successful in getting the math materials you wanted from the library?

6. I wonder how well you remember what you read. Can you tell me about one (the) math item? What was the title or who was the author? What was it about?

7. Do you (not) feel that use of library materials is enjoyable and helpful in achieving your math grade? Why?

8. I see that you did (not) use films or filmstrips? Why (not)?

9. How do you feel about the use of films and filmstrips in comparison to books in math? Why?

10. How about the use of films and filmstrips in comparison to books in history or English?

Appendix F

Interview Questions— Control Group

Since I observed you in your math class, let's talk primarily about math.

1. Do you remember several weeks ago when you had library orientation week and the librarian explained that teachers placed books on reserve?

2. Do you recall your math teacher mentioning that teachers place books on reserve and that such books are charged out by using the request slips?

3. Do you know that for the last few weeks a great many math books and some filmstrips for subfreshmen have been placed on reserve on the shelf behind the circulation desk in the library and that they will be on reserve for another five weeks?
(If answer to #3 is yes, then)

4. How did you know about them and why didn't you use them?
(If answer to #3 is no, then)

4. Didn't anybody in Mr. T's other math class mention them?

5. Whether or not you knew about the reserve books, why didn't you use library materials in math more often?

For one member of control group who borrowed a math book—

6. I noticed that you borrowed one math book during the term. How did you find out about it?
(Go to question #4 experimental scale, and continue to the end.)

For others in control group

6. Do you (not) feel that use of library materials is enjoyable and helpful in achieving your math grade? Why?

165

7. How do you feel about the use of films and filmstrips in comparison to books in math? Why?

8. How about the use of films and filmstrips in comparison to books in history or English?

Appendix G

School Principal's Letter to Parents

December 11, 1969

For several weeks your child has been part of a study relating to method of teaching at the junior high school (sub-freshman) level.

To complete the study, the investigator, Mr. Ronald Blazek of the University of Illinois, must interview each pupil. Because of scheduling difficulties and the desirability of interviewing in a non-school environment, he would like to hold an interview in each child's home.

Mr. Blazek has discussed this interview with all pupils involved in the study. He has submitted to me a schedule for home visits. The date and time for your child's interview are:
The entire interview should take no more than half an hour.

If previous plans make the scheduling date or time inconvenient, please call Mrs. Armstrong at 333-2870 from December 15 through 19.

I appreciate your cooperation in the research being performed at University High School.

Sincerely,

A. F. G.
Principal

AFG/nht

A copy of this letter was sent to the parents of each pupil in the experimental and control groups.

Statistical Applications

MANN-WHITNEY U TEST

Siegel[1] provides a good description of the Mann-Whitney U Test. It is one of the most powerful of the nonparametric tests and is a useful alternative to the parametric t-test when the assumptions regarding a normally distributed population are not observed. The emphasis being on ranks rather than means or scores, therefore it provides the investigator with a statistic which is not influenced unduly by extremes. H_0 indicates that neither group differs appreciably in terms of its distribution of ranks. That is, when individuals in both groups are combined for ranking purposes, the sum of the ranks for each group will be approximately the same. Of course, the greater the difference between groups in the sums of their ranks, the more likely that this difference will be significant.

The formula provided by Siegel is

$$U = n1n2 + \frac{n1\ (n1 - 1)}{2} - R1,$$

or equivalently,

$$U = n1n2 + \frac{n2(n2 + 1)}{2} - R2,$$

where n1 and R1 represent the number of cases and sum of the ranks of the smaller group. In this study, both groups were of the same size (17 pupils) and therefore Re and Rc were substituted for sums of ranks for experimental and control groups, and ne and nc for number of cases. The working formula in the case of a larger rank sum existing in the experimental group as predicted for the test period results is thus:

$$U = nenc + \frac{ne(ne + 1)}{2} - Re.$$

The result is then compared to a table of critical values of U and "if an observed U for a particular n1 ≤ 20 and n2 between 9 and 20 is equal to or less than that value given in the table, H_0 may be rejected at the level of significance indicated at the head of that table."[2]

If, however, the larger rank sum belongs to the control group, the equivalent formula using the control group figures is used. In practical

168

terms this involves only a change of rank sums (Rc for Re), since the number of cases is the same in both groups. In theory, the formula then would be

$$U = nenc + \frac{nc(nc + 1)}{2} - Rc.$$

This formula was used to analyze the results of the pretest in which the sum of the ranks of the control group was greater than that of the experimental group.

CHI SQUARE TEST

In the comparisons of the number of media center patrons where it was thought advisable to employ a statistical test (test period), chi square was suitable. This is a general test which can be used whenever data can be expressed as frequencies in discrete categories. In this study, the pupils were either users or nonusers of the media center. Experimental group users were compared in number to control group users in two ways: first as users of any media which included mathematics and then as users of mathematics materials. The test period was the only period which showed a marked difference between groups in terms of number of users.

The formula for chi square (x^2) as given by Blalock is

$$\text{chi square} = \Sigma \frac{(fo - fe)^2}{fe}$$

where fo and fe refer respectively to the observed and expected frequencies.[3] The expected frequency for each group is based on the observations of the performance of both groups as a whole, dividing in half the total number of users and nonusers and assigning these figures as an expected frequency to each group since both groups have equal membership. Obviously, the greater the difference between observed and expected frequencies, the larger the value of chi square. When this value is larger than that for which chance alone can account, the difference between groups is significant and H_0 may be rejected. Of course, in this case H_0 states that there is no difference between groups in number of users for which chance alone cannot account.

To determine whether the chi square value is significant, one consults the table of critical values of chi square, using the proper figure for degrees of freedom (df). To determine df, one uses the formula $(R - 1)(C - 1)$, where R represents rows and C represents columns needed to set up the table for analysis of the data. This study employs a 2 x 2 table, two columns (users and nonusers), and two rows (experimental and control groups), resulting in one df. A simple descriptive statistic, phi square, is utilized to determine the strength of the relationship between the number of users and the independent variable, and is discussed with respect to table 4 on page 80.

DEPENDENT SAMPLES, MATCHED PAIRS TECHNIQUE

The use of the media center by each member of the experimental group is compared over the three periods and the matched pairs, technique is a form of t-test which is especially appropriate. Variables which could conceivably affect library use are controlled to the greatest degree possible since the three samples consist of the same people. Thus, each pupil's media center use during two of the three periods is compared directly by obtaining his difference score.

> If we use the null hypothesis that there is no difference between the two populations, thereby assuming that the experimental variable has no effect, we can simply hypothesize that the mean of the pair-by-pair differences in the population (μ_D) is zero. The problem then reduces to a single-sample test of the hypothesis that $\mu_D = 0$.[4]

It is recognized by the investigator that the effective application of any parametric statistic presupposes the assumptions of a normally distributed population as well as random selection of samples. This is always a problem when N, the total number of cases, is small. In this case, however, there is no reason to think that the population of differences in circulation rate from one given period of time to another should be significantly changed when the same group of pupils is compared. That is, unless a variable had been introduced which effected a change in the population of media center users from one period to the next. This, of course, was the premise to be tested.

This technique, therefore, is regarded as the best combination of suitability and rigor in treating the data concerning the experimental group. It focuses on the test period which is compared to each of the other two periods to determine whether or not the differences are significant. Moreover, full advantage is taken for the first time of the interval scale data present in library circulation, and the mean is considered as the basis for judgment.

The formula given by Blalock[5] to find the significance of the differences is:

$$t = \frac{\overline{X}_D - \mu_D}{s_D/\sqrt{N-1}}.$$

The mean of the sample difference, represented by $\overline{X}_D$, is found by adding the differences between periods for each pupil and dividing by N.

The sample standard deviation of differences (s_D) is found by sub-tracting $\overline{X}_D$ from the individual difference score for each pupil, squaring the result, summing these figures for all pupils, dividing by N, and taking the square root of the result. H_0 states that the mean of the differences in the population, μ_D, is zero. This is tested when zero value is assigned to it in the formula. Obviously, the greater the value of $\overline{X}_D$, the greater the departure from the hypothetical μ_D. When the difference is great enough to be significant, H_0 is rejected.

The t distribution is used with $N - 1$ or in this case 16 df, providing the basis for determining the critical value needed to reject H_0. The 0.05 significance level again is used, employing a one-tailed test since direction of difference is predicted. Of importance is the use of mean weekly circulation data for each pupil for each of the three test periods for purposes of comparison. This was necessary since the test period was of longer duration than were the pretest and post-test, and raw circulation figures would be biased in favor of the test period.

KENDALL'S TAU

Hays[6] provides Kendall's formula for tau or the apparent degree of agreement between two variable rankings in these terms:

$$\text{Tau} = \frac{S}{\sqrt{\left\{\frac{N(N-1) - T1}{2}\right\}\left\{\frac{N(N-1) - T2}{2}\right\}}}$$

The figure for S is representative of the order of agreement between the rankings as acquired through tables 40–43 of the original study,[7] in which one variable is ranked by columns and the other by rows. $S+$ is tabulated by counting the number of cases to the right and below every cell (each cell being weighted by its frequency or number of cases), $S-$ is computed in exactly the same way except that the number of cases to the left and below a given cell are counted. Subtracting $S-$ from $S+$ provides a value for S.

T1 and T2 are corrections for tied scores within the ranks of each variable which serve to reduce the size of the denominator in the equation, and thereby result in slightly higher taus or correlation coefficients.

$$T1 = \frac{nj(nj - 1)}{2}$$

where nj is the marginal total for column j.

$$T2 = \frac{nk(nk - 1)}{2}$$

where nk is the marginal total for row k. It should be clear that the greater

171

the size of S in proportion to the denominator, the greater the resulting tau or correlation.

Kendall's test of significance is also presented by Hays, and requires the computations of the sampling variance of S as the first step.

Sampling Variance =

$$\frac{N(N-1)(2N+5) - \Sigma nj(nj-1)(2nj+5) - \Sigma nk(nk-1)(2nk+5)}{18}$$

$$+\frac{[\Sigma nj(nj-1)(nj-2)][\Sigma nk-1)(nk-2)]}{9(N)(N-1)(N-2)}$$

$$+\frac{[\Sigma nj(nj-1)][\Sigma(nk)(nk-1)]}{2(N)(N-1)}.$$

This computation of the sampling variance is performed when ties exist and enables one to obtain the Z score by the simple formula,

$$Z = \frac{S}{\text{Standard error}}.$$

Of course, this is done after taking the square root of the sampling variance (standard error). Since there are frequent ties within the ranks, a correction for continuity is given by Kendall (S — 1 in the case of positive S or S+1 in the case of negative S).[8] In these correlational analyses, H_0 indicates that there is no association between the two variables for which chance alone cannot account. The level of significance needed for rejection of H_0 is again 0.05.

Notes

1. Sidney Siegel, *Nonparametric Statistics for the Behavioral Sciences* (New York: McGraw-Hill, 1956), pp. 116–26.

2. Ibid., p. 119.

3. Hubert M. Blalock, *Social Statistics* (2d ed.; New York: McGraw-Hill, 1972), p. 276.

4. Ibid., p. 233.

5. Ibid., p. 235.

6. William L. Hays, *Statistics for Psychologists* (New York: Holt, 1963), p. 654.

7. Ronald D. Blazek, "Teacher Utilization of Nonrequired Library Materials in Mathematics and the Effect on Pupil Use" (Unpublished Ph.D. dissertation, Univ. of Illinois, 1971).

8. Maurice G. Kendall, *Rank Correlation Methods* (London, Eng.: Griffin, 1962), p. 54.

Selected Bibliography

Dissertations and Theses

Barth, Edward Walter. "The Relationship between Selected Teaching Structures and the Activities of Media Centers in Public Senior High Schools in the State of Maryland." Ed.D. dissertation, George Washington Univ., 1971. 222p.

Bishop, Martha Dell. "Identification of Valuable Learning Experiences in Centralized Elementary School Libraries." Ed.D. dissertation, George Peabody College for Teachers, 1963. 147p.

Blazek, Ronald David. "Teacher Utilization of Nonrequired Library Materials in Mathematics and the Effect on Pupil Use." Ph.D. dissertation, Univ. of Illinois, 1971. 283p.

Christison, Milton Robert. "An Examination of Selected Variables Associated with Elementary Instructional Material Centers." Ph.D. dissertation, Univ. of Wisconsin, 1973. 108p.

Clayton, Howard. "An Investigation of Various Social and Economic Factors Influencing Student Use of One College Library." Ph.D. dissertation, Univ. of Oklahoma, 1965. 140p.

Cogan, Morris L. "The Relation of the Behavior of Teachers to the Productive Behavior of Their Pupils." Ed.D. dissertation, Harvard Univ., 1954.

Cyphert, Frederick R. "Current Practice in the Use of the Library in Selected Junior High Schools in Pennsylvania." Ed.D. dissertation, Univ. of Pittsburgh, 1957. 234p.

Donnelly, Edward Joseph. "The Organization and Administration of Instructional Materials Centers in Selected High Schools." Ed.D. dissertation, Univ. of Nebraska, 1965. 186p.

Ducat, Sister Mary Peter Claver. "Student and Faculty Use of the Library in Three Secondary Schools." Ph.D. dissertation, Columbia Univ., 1960. 302p.

Fortin, Clifford Charles. "The Relation of Certain Personal and Environmental Characteristics of School Librarians to Their Life Values and Work Satisfactions." Ph.D. dissertation, Univ. of Minnesota, 1970. 124p.

Gengler, Charles Richard. "A Study of Selected Problem Solving Skills Comparing Teacher Instructed Students with Librarian-Teacher Instructed Students." Ed.D. dissertation, Univ. of Oregon, 1965. 326p.

Graham, Robert James. "The Impact of Title II of the Elementary and Secondary Education Act of 1965 on Selected Michigan High Schools." Ed.D. dissertation, Univ. of Michigan, 1969. 187p.

Grassmeyer, Donald Leroy. "The Organization and Administration of Instructional Materials Centers in Selected Junior High Schools." Ed.D. dissertation, Univ. of Nebraska, 1966. 120p.

Greve, Clyde Leroy. "The Relationship of the Availability of Libraries to the Academic Achievement of Iowa High School Seniors." Ph.D. dissertation, Univ. of Denver, 1974. 130p.

Hagrasy, Saad Mohammed el-. "The Teacher's Role in Library Service." Ph.D. dissertation, Rutgers Univ., 1961. 275p.

Hall, Sedley Duane. "A Comparative Study of Two Types of Organization of Instructional Materials Centers." Ed.D. dissertation, Univ. of Nebraska Teachers College, 1963. 118p.

Hannigan, Jane Anne Therese. "Reading, Viewing, and Listening Characteristics of Academically Talented Students." Ph.D. dissertation, Columbia Univ. 1969, 740p.

Hempstead, John Orson. "Media and the Learner: The Influence of Media-Message Components on Students' Recall and Attitudes toward the Learning Experience." Ph.D. dissertation, Univ. of Wisconsin, 1973. 144p.

Henry, Marion. "A Study of Library Services in the Public Schools of Texas." Ph.D. dissertation, Syracuse Univ., 1972. 237p.

Hostrop, Richard. "The Relationship of Academic Success and Selected Other Factors to Student Use of Library Materials at College of the Desert." Ed.D. dissertation, Univ. of California at Los Angeles, 1966. 317p.

Holzerbein, Deanne Basler. "The Contribution of School Media Programs to Elementary and Secondary Education as Portrayed in Professional Journals Available to School Administrators from 1960–69." Ph.D. dissertation, Univ. of Michigan, 1971. 262p.

Jay, Hilda Lease. "Increasing the Use of Secondary School Libraries as a Teaching Tool." Ed.D. dissertation, New York Univ., 1970. 134p.

Jetter, Margaret Ann. "The Roles of the School Library Media Specialist in the Future: A Delphi Study." Ph.D. dissertation, Michigan State Univ., 1972. 275p.

King, Kenneth Lee. "An Evaluation of Teacher Utilization of Selected Educational Media in Relation to the Level of Sophistication of the Educational Media Program in Selected Oklahoma Public Schools." Ed.D. dissertation, Univ. of Oklahoma, 1969. 223p.

Knapp, Patricia B. "Role of the Library of a Given College in Implementing the Course and Non-Course Objectives of the College." Ph.D. dissertation, Univ. of Chicago, 1957. 298p.

Lacock, Donald Wayne. "The Media Specialist and Tasks Related to the Design, Production and Utilization of Instructional Materials." Ed.D. dissertation, Univ. of Nebraska, 1971. 174p.

Loertscher, David Mickers. "Media Center Services to Teachers in Indiana Senior High Schools, 1972–1973." Ph.D. dissertation, Indiana Univ., 1973. 158p.

Mack, Edna B. "The School Library's Contribution to the Total Educational Program of the School: A Content Analysis of Selected Periodicals in the Field of Education." Ph.D. dissertation, Univ. of Michigan, 1957. 378p.

McMillen, Ralph Donnelly. "An Analysis of Library Programs and a Determination of the Educational Justification of These Programs in Selected

Elementary Schools of Ohio." Ed.D. dissertation, Western Reserve Univ., 1965. 250p.

Madaus, James Richard. "Curriculum Involvement, Teaching Structures, and Personality Factors of Librarians in School Media Programs." Ph.D. dissertation, Univ. of Texas at Austin, 1974. 123p.

Mehit, George. "Effects of Type of Library Service upon Utilization of Books by Sixth Grade Pupils in Selected County Elementary Schools of Northeastern Ohio." Ed.D. dissertation, Western Reserve Univ., 1965. 206p.

Miller, Rosalind Elaine. "Instructional Materials Centers as Related to Types of Learning: The Application of Gagné's Learning Principles to Media Stimulus." Ph.D. dissertation, St. Louis Univ., 1972. 145p.

Replogle, James R. "The Relation of Teacher-Pupil Profile Pattern Similarities on Measures by Interest and Personality to Grades and Perceived Compatibility." Ed.D. dissertation, Lehigh Univ., 1968. 120p.

Schmitz, Eugenia. "A Study of the Library Book Collections in Mathematics and the Physical Sciences in 54 Michigan High Schools Accredited by the North Central Association of Colleges and Secondary Schools." Ph.D. dissertation, Univ. of Michigan, 1966. 1182p.

Thomason, Ella Nevada Wallis. "An Investigation of Student Attitudes toward and Utilization of Total Media Facilities in Public Junior College Libraries in Texas." Ph.D. dissertation, Univ. of Colorado, 1972. 216p.

Tielke, Elton Fritz. "A Study of the Relationship of Selected Environmental Factors to the Development of Elementary School Libraries." Ed.D. dissertation, Univ. of Texas, 1968. 319p.

Wert, Lucille Mathena. "Library Education and High School Library Services." Ph.D. dissertation, Univ. of Illinois, 1970. 364p.

Woods, William. "Factors Influencing Student Library Use: An Analysis of Studies." Master's thesis, Univ. of Chicago, 1965. 52p.

Yarling, James Robert. "Children's Understandings and Use of Selected Library-Related Skills in Two Elementary Schools, One with and One without a Centralized Library." Ed.D. dissertation, Ball State Univ., 1968. 210p.

Books and Monographs

Barnes, Fred P. *Research for the Practitioner in Education.* Washington, DC: National Education Assn., 1964. 141p.

Blalock, Hubert M. *Social Statistics.* 2d ed. New York: McGraw-Hill, 1972. 583p.

Bruner, Jerome S. *The Process of Education.* Cambridge, Mass.: Harvard Univ. Pr., 1960. 97p.

Flanders, Ned A. *Teacher Influence, Pupil Attitudes, and Achievement.* (Cooperative Research Monograph, no. 12) Washington, DC: Gov. Print. Off., 1965. 126p.

French, John R. P., and Raven, Bertrand. "The Bases of Social Power," *in* Dorwin Cartwright and Alvin Zander, eds., *Group Dynamics Research and Theory,* pp. 259–69. New York: Harper, 1968.

Johnson, Donald M., and Smith, Henry C. "Democratic Leadership in the College Classroom," in *Psychological Monographs,* (v. 67, no. 11) Menasha, Wis.: American Psychological Assn., 1953. 20p.

Bibliography

Knapp, Patricia B. *College Teaching and the College Library.* (ACRL Monographs, no. 23) Chicago: American Library Assn., 1959. 110p.
Krumboltz, J. D., and Farquhar, William W. "The Effects of Three Teaching Methods on Achievement and Motivational Outcomes in a How-to-Study Course," in *Psychological Monographs.* (v. 71, no. 14) Washington, DC: American Psychological Assn., 1957. 26p.
Lowrie, Jean. "A Review of Research in School Librarianship," in Herbert Goldhor, ed., *Research Methods in Librarianship: Measurement and Evaluation.* (Monograph no. 8) Champaign, Ill.: Univ. of Illinois Graduate School of Library Science, 1968. pp. 51–69.
National Education Assn., Research Div. *The Secondary-School Teacher and Library Services.* (Research monograph 1958-M1) Washington, DC: The Association, 1958. 37p.
Siegel, Sidney. *Nonparametric Statistics for the Behavioral Sciences.* New York: McGraw-Hill, 1956. 312p.
Skinner, B. F. *The Technology of Teaching.* New York: Appleton, 1968. 271p.

1296-6
5-22